Advance Praise for

Life by the Cup

"*Life by the Cup* is a delicious and engaging book that will inspire and guide you. It offers a powerful road map for success in life, work, and love. Within the pages are many gems that ensure you have the tools to live your dreams."

—Marci Shimoff, author of *Happy for No Reason: 7 Steps to Being Happy from the Inside Out*

"Zhena's new book opens a delicious world where expansion and fulfillment can occur one cup at a time. She shows you how caring for your deep self fuels your deepest success in all aspects of your life. Whether you are a mother, entrepreneur, or simply passionate about expressing your creative self most fully, *Life by the Cup* serves delectable sips of magic."

—Kathlyn Hendricks, coauthor of *Conscious Loving: The Journey to Co-Commitment*

"I love this book! Zhena's journey and the lessons she shares in *Life by the Cup* will inspire and empower women to start businesses that matter and can change the world."

—Cynthia Kersey, chief humanitarian officer of Unstoppable Foundation

"It wasn't enough for Zhena to create one of the hottest brands in the tea industry; she did it by forging a soulful, life-changing partnership with tea farmers halfway around the world. And now, through this remarkable book, she's given us all a seat next to her on this magical journey. Zhena reminds us that we each can make a difference in the world through something as simple and delicious as a cup of tea."

—Paul Rice, president and CEO of Fair Trade USA

"*Life by the Cup* is a world-changing, unique, and beautifully written book that will benefit every aspect of the reader's life. Zhena Muzyka reflects on her complex and inspirational life by artfully weaving delightful tea antidotes, unforgettable personal stories, and her savvy business prowess. I laughed, sobbed, and was inspired to make the world a better place while reading *Life by the Cup* over many delicious cups of tea. Muzyka inspires readers to create more meaningful rituals in their daily lives and to become the most deeply joyful, fearless, and empowered version of themselves."

— **Erin Cox**, enlightened business strategist and bestselling author of *One Hot Mama: The Guide to Getting Your Mind and Body Back After Baby*

"Recipes for overcoming adversity swirl through these pages like the inspiriting ingredients in Zhena's tea concoctions. I sipped from her book every night at bedtime, and invariably solutions for my own life steeped in my dreams."

— **Terri Jentz**, author of *Strange Piece of Paradise*

Life by the Cup

Life by the Cup

Ingredients for a Purpose-Filled Life
of Bottomless Happiness and
Limitless Success

Founder, Zhena's Gypsy Tea

ATRIA BOOKS

New York London Toronto Sydney New Delhi

ATRIA BOOKS

A Division of Simon & Schuster, Inc.
1230 Avenue of the Americas
New York, NY 10020

First Atria Books hardcover edition June 2014

ATRIA BOOKS and colophon are trademarks of Simon & Schuster, Inc.

For information about special discounts for bulk purchases, please contact Simon & Schuster Special Sales at 1-866-506-1949 or business@simonandschuster.com.

The Simon & Schuster Speakers Bureau can bring authors to your live event. For more information or to book an event, contact the Simon & Schuster Speakers Bureau at 1-866-248-3049 or visit our website at www.simonspeakers.com.

Book design by Ellen R. Sasahara
Jacket design by Connie Gabbert
Jacket art © Masson/Shutterstock; © primpopiano/Shutterstock;
© kanate/Shutterstock; © Elena Schweitzer/Shutterstock

Manufactured in the United States of America

10 9 8 7 6 5 4 3 2 1

Library of Congress Cataloging-in-Publication Data

Muzyka, Zhena.
   Life by the cup: ingredients for a purpose-filled life of bottomless happiness and limitless success / Zhena Muzyka.
         pages cm
   Includes index.
   1. Muzyka, Zhena. 2. Zhena's Gypsy Tea Company. 3. Businesswomen—United States—Biography. 4. Tea trade—United States—History. 5. Success in business—United States. 6. Self-realization. I. Title.
   HD9198.U54Z446 2014
   338.7'66394092—dc23
   [B]
                         2013047967

ISBN 978-1-4767-5960-9
ISBN 978-1-4767-5964-7 (ebook)

For Sage—You inspire me daily

Contents

ix

Foreword

One day I was talking with some girlfriends about how I wanted to write an inspirational book that people could read in the time it took to have a cup of tea. I would tell the stories of my experiences building a company as a single-mom entrepreneur and also help readers see that a simple cup of tea can be a daily ritual for personal transformation and growth.

Dyana said, "Make the chapters short enough to sip!"

So, knowing how busy everyone is these days, I share my insights in this book in a new kind of way—by the cup. As women, mothers, career builders, world changers, wives, and dreamers, we need to find our individual mission as well as our collective mission. It's important to find ourselves and then gather together, share what we learn, support one another, and *love* our work.

I started my company with nothing but the burning desire to provide a good and healthful life for my sick newborn son, but I found so much more. When my world seemed limited, hemmed in by impenetrable walls, tea, hope, and my active dreams saved my son, Sage, and me. I took responsibility for someone other than myself and grew into a person Sage could count on. I got serious about my life, which was now *our* life.

I had to ask big questions, seek meaningful answers, grow my faith in ways I never knew imaginable, and step into the role of a lifetime—mom, tea maker, and, eventually, fair-trade activist. My family came to include the tea workers who harvested the precious organic leaves and buds that I blended and sold. We are all connected.

Within these pages you'll read about my hardest-won insights, life lessons that are meant to inspire you to find and follow your own passion. I encourage you to allow all the mistakes you will make in the course of finding your path to be part of your own repertoire of life lessons, for these lessons will shape your destiny. The beloved transformational teacher Byron Katie says, "Business grows us," and she couldn't be more right. Motherhood gave birth to a new strength in me, hardship carved me into a mom my son could count on, and my mission to bring prosperity to tea workers half a world away kept me going even when bankruptcy loomed.

I want to inspire you to be audacious in your dreams and committed to your values—no matter how messy your path may become. Know that when God gives you lemons, you can make tea (or cupcakes, jewelry, art, or love . . .). Happiness is not born from playing it safe. Inspiration is abundant—it's yours for the taking—and it sometimes comes from the most unexpected places.

Just as I find the greatest pleasure in serving others a cup of tea, I have found great pleasure in storytelling—it's hereditary, in my Gypsy blood. I invite you to take some quiet time out of the day for ritual. Make yourself a cup of tea and sit down with this book to enjoy a few moments for yourself. Take a journey with me. The stories and recipes are dedicated to you and your personal quest to plumb the depths of your potential. Let's sip to finding and fulfilling those big destinies! Whatever your profession, whether you're working or not, you will find little gems in these pages that will reassure you of your imminent success.

If I can do what I do—and I was as unlikely an entrepreneur as could be—*you* can absolutely and irrefutably do *anything*. Just know that when life is overwhelming, it is much more manageable when you take it one cup at a time. Let's have one together now.

Life by the Cup

Introduction

If you can find a path with no obstacles,
it probably doesn't lead anywhere.

—FRANK A. CLARK

December 1, 1999
Ojai, California

As I lifted the cup of tea to my nose, inhaling the steamy, sweet scent, anticipating my first sip, I saw Kevin, the utility man, tiptoeing into the yard through the side gate like a cat burglar. Looking over the rim of my cup, through the faint waves of circling steam, I fixed my gaze on him.

He was so focused on reaching our fuse box that he didn't see me sitting only a dozen feet away on the front porch steps, bundled up in an old red Indian blanket, warming my face in the distant morning sun.

Quietly putting the cup down on the weathered porch, I watched as he neared the back of the house. Standing as quickly as I could without setting off a symphony of creaks in the old wooden steps, I balanced my enormously pregnant belly and stepped onto the dead grass, making my way over to where Kevin was about to close off the valve with his wrench, which would leave me without precious fuel to heat my one-room cabin or cook my daily lentils, rice, and tea. I cornered him and yelled, "Hey!"

He jumped and almost dropped the tool. He looked over at me, raising his shoulders to his ears, grimacing as if he thought I would hit him. "If *you* do that, my baby and I will *freeze to death* and you'll have to sleep at night knowing what you did!" I pointed at my nine-month pregnant belly for good measure.

He looked at me sideways. It wasn't the first time we had met and wouldn't be our last.

I smiled nervously, feeling bad to have scared him. "In all seriousness, Kevin, you know I am going to pay the bill, so why come out here and do this to me?" I smiled again, trying to be charming.

"It's four months past due," he pleaded. "You're going to get me fired!"

"Look," I said, "I'm about to give birth, then I can get a job. Can you just wait for a couple of weeks, tell your boss I have a scary dog or something? Anything?"

He looked at me for a few hard beats before dropping his shoulders. "You're gonna have to do something, you know. The county has programs . . ."

I knew. I was about to have a kid and my only assets were a rusted-out, thirty-year-old car with no driver's window and perpetually less than ten bucks in my bank account. How does one go about "doing something" when there is so much *surviving* to do?

"People don't hire pregnant ladies, you know," I told him, squinting back my tears.

He shook his head and stomped back up the driveway and onto the worn-out canyon road, thankfully without cutting off our power.

Somewhere along the line, God and I had gotten our wires crossed. I blamed my impulsive nature and sometimes believed that my destiny had come and gone already. I felt like I had missed my boat. I was a broke, pregnant twenty-four-year-old college dropout, fending off a kindly utility man.

I headed back to the front porch feeling seasick. To steady myself, I grabbed my anchor, that simple cup of tea.

I had been an honors student, a full scholarship recipient, a girl with so much "promise." Then I followed one too many yearnings in my Gypsy blood and took off. I dropped out of college, headed to Peru, studied herbal medicine, got married and divorced, all the while earning my keep by making healing herbal concoctions and reading palms like my Roma Gypsy family in the Ukraine once had.

This hadn't been my plan, having a baby on my own at twenty-four. I was heartbroken over the circumstance. I must have sat there for a long time, because when I took another sip of tea, it was ice-cold.

I begged out loud, "God, you have to help me here! Tell me what to do!" Silence.

After a few beats, the odd answer that entered my mind as I looked out at the mountains was two mismatched words, "Gypsy . . ." and then "tea."

"Seriously!?" I yelled, looking into my teacup as if God presided in there.

I thought my mind was playing tricks on me. After all, I was a Gypsy girl drinking tea, so the idea had to have come from my desperate mind, not from the Almighty. But the idea of taking my heritage, my deep love of botanicals, and my passion for crafting healing gifts became more than just a momentary impulse. It became motivation to build something beautiful that mattered in the world.

Sage, my beautiful baby boy, was born with a life-threatening kidney defect, and we spent weeks in hospital waiting rooms and surgery centers. In between prayers and tears, I'd close my eyes to escape the fear of potentially losing my precious child. My mind conjured visions of children laughing as their moms sipped from colorful teacups and other women danced around them in brightly hued costumes. Beautiful Gypsy women proudly displayed their art, handmade jewelry, and palm-reading wisdom with kind smiles across their faces. There were cups of tea everywhere, filled with potions that I had blended from inspirations of famous perfumes I loved—floral flavors made for spiritual healing. These potions would soothe mothers' worries, inspire love in lonely people, encourage girls' ambitions, and calm everyone's nerves, bringing them together in a sort of tea communion. It was all there in my mind's seeking eye. These images of Gypsy-themed tea parties grew into hope.

A coping method, a promise, a dream—tea became all of those things to me.

1

The Carving of the Cup

A Cup of Capacity

Deep unspeakable suffering may well be called a baptism,
a regeneration, the initiation into a new state.

—GEORGE ELIOT

Inspiration: The beauty of a cup. The sensory delight of tea has much to do with the vessel it's served in. I love a cup I can wrap both hands around as I raise it to my lips. A cup is a touchstone of tranquility, of warmth and nourishment. It is also a measure of capacity, for how much a cup can hold is critical for anchoring our experience. The thinness of a cup's walls conveys the craftsmanship and mindfulness that went into its making. If you truly notice the cup you drink from, you create a meaningful ritual that infuses your tea drinking and your life.

My signature teacup is hand-painted like a Ukrainian Easter egg in rich hues of burgundy, pink, forest green, midnight blue, and golden egg-yolk yellow. It belonged to Grandma Maria, my

Gypsy grandmother from Ukraine. It holds a lot of tea, as well as hundreds of memories of a woman whose life was hard yet full of passion and spirit.

A young Tibetan refugee couple told me of their harrowing escape from Chinese-occupied Tibet to India. Their faces remained peaceful as they recounted fleeing from their home and leaving their family, practically barefoot, through the icy Himalayas, fending off frostbite, falling victim to snow blindness, and narrowly surviving the violent fury of an avalanche. Hearing their story when I was age twenty-two, I couldn't comprehend how they could be so serene. The horrors they'd suffered reminded me of Grandma Maria's trials when she fled Stalin's regime, after having survived years in a concentration camp, forced famines, and two decades of war on her people, the Gypsies. She had walked in a subzero winter from eastern Ukraine to Germany in order to flee Stalin's sinister genocide.

When I met the Tibetan couple, I was grieving my grandmother's death. I had moved to Ojai to write a book about her, to try to record her travails and honor her struggles. The Tibetans' story filled me with outrage that this kind of injustice was still happening.

I burst out, "How are you so calm? They took everything from you! Aren't you angry?"

"No, the pain has a meaning," the young man said. His kind-eyed wife nodded and put her hand on his. "You see," he continued, "when we are born, we are a rough block of wood. The pain we go through and feel as we move through this life, it is the hand of God carving us, shaping us. The carving feels bad, but it is forming us into a cup that can hold more and more as each stroke of pain carves another rough piece of us away. And then we have more and more space to hold things: love, happiness, nature, and beauty."

Grandma Maria embodied this idea, even after all the inhumanity she'd seen and experienced. Instead of being bitter, she had a fathomless capacity for love and healing.

This realization made me remember my own most trying experiences; the heartbreak I felt at failing others and myself was always replaced somehow by new understanding. I imagined the hand of God shaping me, deepening me, refining me. Blame was washed away. I was not a victim but a vessel, being artfully sculpted for my future.

"Eventually," he said softly, "the walls of the cup get thinner and thinner until they disappear and you spill into the space beyond the cup. You become one with all. You become life."

As he spoke, all hardships were reframed. Well . . . until the real carving began.

After my son was born, Sage was often sick with what the doctor at first thought was colic—but at four weeks old, he was diagnosed with kidney failure. Within hours, Sage was getting shots of radioactive isotopes in order to have a nuclear medicine scan to see how far gone his kidneys were. Then he was prepped for surgery. His tiny legs kicked in protest and my own hot tears burned streaks on my face.

The image of the cup came back to me. Pain dealt to those who can defend themselves or escape it is one thing, but my baby didn't know what was happening to him. His pain was senseless, and my inability to help him was crushing me. I had to strengthen myself in order to protect him.

The surgery went smoothly and, in the recovery room, I cupped Sage's little head and held his feet, afraid to take my eyes off him.

A nurse entered the room and said, "We're going to pull these curtains around you and the baby so we can bring in another patient."

"What if they hear me?" I worried. "I'm kind of crying a lot."

"Oh, don't worry," she said. "Cry as much as you need to. It's good for you."

Soon I heard voices as another bed was wheeled into the room. A series of IVs and monitoring machines chirped to life.

Sage continued to sleep peacefully, no longer than my forearm, so small.

Although I couldn't see the other mother behind the curtain, I felt connected to her. I could hear her take deep breaths and flip the pages of a book. I heard her feel for something in her purse, then a ChapStick dropped on the floor and her hand appeared under the curtain reaching for it. She let out another deep breath.

"Hi," I ventured.

"Hi," she returned.

"I'm Zhena, and my son Sage is in here. He's four weeks old."

"Oh, how sweet. I'm Meredith. My son, Cody, is twelve."

I said, "He's quiet."

"Yes, he's out," she said.

"Is it okay to ask why he's here?"

"Sure. He doesn't have the enzyme to digest food, so we feed him through an IV, but this week the IV wasn't absorbing and so he's not getting any nutrients."

Her voice was even, calm, but I could feel her sadness.

"What's happening with Sage?"

"It's his kidneys. The doctors had to make a hole in his bladder. He'll be this way until he's three or so, then they can rebuild his system and close him up." My stomach clenched as I said the words aloud for the first time.

"They are great here, such good doctors. It sounds like he's going to be fine."

"Will you have to feed Cody with IVs forever?" I asked.

"I hope not, but it's been twelve years and the enzyme therapies aren't working yet."

"Has he ever tasted food?" I asked.

"No, she said, "not yet, but hopefully soon."

I let this sink in. She had managed to witness his pain and bear her own for so long. We had only begun our fight. Where was I going to find the strength to deal with Sage's illness?

Eventually, I left Sage long enough to search out some juice to drink. The pediatric ward was full of parents pacing, talking on cell phones, pressing the nurses for answers, reading to their recovering kids, loving them with every breath, every word, every look, fighting for them with every fiber.

Two weeks later, back in our little cabin, I took down from the shelf Grandma Maria's cup. It was the only physical remnant of her I had, and just the sight of it was comforting. On the porch, I sipped tea from it as the sun lit the canyon pink and gold. The cup was full of her memory—the soft sounds of her praying, the Gypsy fireside songs she sang, and childhood lessons in her magical garden where she showed me the soil's ability to sustain us. She had lost so much, and yet her love was profound enough to sustain me long after she'd left this world.

As the sun went down on those terrible two weeks, I realized that Sage's and my life had been altered, carved wider, opened up for a miracle. I was broken open, and into all that new space seeped Big Love, faith, and the fierceness I needed in order to create a life for my son. Without the pain we had just been through, I might have never discovered these reserves of strength.

The Carving of Your Cup

Mantra of the Cup: I breathe through pain. As it moves through and out of me, it gives me a greater capacity to love.

Pain is the messenger of change. It demands that we grow, endure, and heal. Ultimately, pain transforms us and points us to our true north—our calling. Pain is the fire that makes us into diamonds. It pressurizes our rough, uncut, dark angles into glistening reflectors of our soul's light.

There is no permanent cure for pain. It's a powerful force that returns to us periodically, and whenever it does, it can upend our lives and send us into a tailspin. Through the years, I've sought ways to make my own and others' pain go away, from fighting, complaining, medicating, and hiding to shopping, drinking, and eating too much. Nothing worked for very long.

Many years later, I found and became a practitioner of Vipassana meditation, or insight meditation, the method taught by Buddha. Insight meditation is like a "technology" to end the perpetuating of sadness. It aids our recovery from pain by making us sit still and steady through it, allowing God's hand to carve us into vessels of love and compassion. Buddha himself had realized that he could not cope with seeing and feeling the pain and suffering in the world. Rather than trying to make pain go away or "cure" it, he discovered that meditation moves us right into the eye of its storm, where we find peace and insight.

In my first silent retreat, a lot of pain rose up in unbearable waves. My knees hurt, and so did my back, my head, and my heart. I was also angry and railing against the suffering and injustice in the world, at poverty, pollution, war, and greed. I would remember Sage's cries of pain and want to jump off my meditation cushion, punch holes in walls, and scream in his defense. I wanted to rumble, to show pain who was boss. But I had to sit through it, silently. No picking up the phone to cry to my mom, no going out for a drink with girlfriends, and no complaining to my brothers about how unfair life was. Silence and sitting still were all that was allowed.

Then, as if by a miracle, one afternoon when I thought I couldn't sit any longer, I realized that the pain of sitting was a sensation like pleasure. I had spent my whole life running toward pleasure and away from pain, leaving me never in the moment but always in transit. This catharsis let me see that I was always craving, never content. Anger and sharp pains in my body melted into deep sadness and I silently cried. In between sits, I walked to and from my dorm sobbing, wanting so badly to talk away the anguish, but the vow of silence made it impossible even to make eye contact with other meditators. Without an audience, without a means of running away, I found that the pain started to lose steam and diminish. In its place many sensations arose: relief, joy, curiosity. Then pain, frustration, and anger again. The emotions were taking turns trying to get my attention, but I listened to the meditation teacher who advised us to stop reacting to the sensations and just notice each one as it came up, name it as calmly as we could, and then let it go. Eventually, after several days of silence and ten hours a day of sitting in a novice's version of equanimity, I felt the pain finally become manageable, because I stopped trying to manage it.

When other meditators and I were given the "all clear" to start talking again, all I could do was laugh. People asked me about my experience, but there were no words to describe the lightness I finally felt, just my belly-deep guffaw. The teachers, whom I had dubbed the "meditation police" during those many rough days, looked on as I sat on my cushion hee-hawing with happy tears streaking my face. My attachment to the pain had been the weight I was carrying, so much greater than the pain itself. The heavier the pain, the brighter the light once the pain is released.

I rushed home to Sage, and instead of being all-serious-mom-businesswoman-keep-it-together-or-the-world-will-end-oh-and-don't-smile-just-in-case-something-scary-happens-again, I held him, throwing him up in the air, tickling him, rolling on the ground with him, looking deeply into his lucid little eyes, and as we giggled, we filled his kidneys with the healing light that now poured from my heart, the very light that grew from the seeds pain had planted deep in the soil of my soul.

Exercise: Sit Steady, Scan, and See

First, find a private place to sit quietly, where you're least likely to be interrupted. (I've used the bathroom floor, the backseat of my car, my bed, a cave at the beach, a rock on a quiet trail.) Then find a pillow or chair to sit on. You'll need a digital timer (you can use a kitchen timer or the one on your phone, but turn off your wireless so you aren't tempted to check messages when the going gets tough).

1. Sit cross-legged or comfortably on your chair or pillow.

2. Set your timer for eleven minutes (twenty-two if you can spare them). You can always work up to more time. Doing this daily is ideal and most effective, even if five minutes is all you have.

3. Close your eyes and breathe deeply in and out through your nose. Be aware of the breath entering and leaving your nostrils. Focus on the sensation of the skin just under your nose as the breath enters and leaves your nostrils. Focus. Each time your mind wanders, gently return it to the sensation of your breath entering a leaving your nose. One of my mentors says that when your mind wanders, it's like a kitten escaping a box—no need to get mad at the kitten, just gently put it back in the box!

4. Take your focus from the area under your nose and scan your body, from your head down to your toes. Start with the top of your head and methodically go into each muscle of your face, neck, shoulders, arms, hands, chest, back, solar plexus, abdomen, hips, thighs, knees, calves, ankles, feet, and toes. Notice any sensation in any part of your body but do not linger in any one spot. See the sensation, observe it without judging it, and then keep scanning. Observe each sensation of your body as if you

are a nurse observing a patient—no judgment, just quiet observation, acceptance, and then on to the next part of the body.

5. Reverse your scan: starting at your toes, move up through your feet, ankles, calves, knees, thighs, hips, abdomen, solar plexus, back, chest, hands, arms, shoulders, neck, chin, mouth, cheeks, nose, eyes, forehead, and up to the top of the head.

6. Repeat steps 4 and 5. Whenever a sensation comes up, observe and name it in your mind. Whenever an emotion comes up, observe and name it in your mind. If your knee hurts, simply name it "pain"; if you're worrying, name it "worrying." And keep going, naming each sensation without attaching to it. The key is to maintain your momentum through the scanning and observing.

7. When the timer goes off, take one final deep breath and release it slowly. Bring your attention back to your heart and visualize your heart opening up; see a bright light glowing there.

Doing this practice consistently peels away the layers of reactions we automatically engage in when fear and pain arise. By observing, naming, and moving on, you begin to see pain and pleasure as impermanent sensations. By observing them without glomming on to the story, by not becoming attached to them, you liberate yourself from running toward pleasure or away from pain and are free to stand fully in the face of your entire life. You are free to become lighter, happier, and more spacious. The power that pain has over you will slowly diminish, giving way to new possibilities in your body and mind. What is left is more of you, accessible and present to your beautiful life and all the joy it generously brings.

> The secret of health for both mind and body is not
> to mourn for the past, nor to worry about the future,
> but to live the present moment wisely and earnestly.
>
> —BUDDHA

2

Pride Cannot Feed a Baby

A Cup of Lentils, Fennel Seeds, and Chamomile Blossoms

To help all created things, that is the measure of all
our responsibility; to be helped by all, that is
the measure of our hope.

—GERALD VANN

Inspiration: Italian chamomile. Chamomile blossoms sprinkle the pathway to my front porch like starry lights. The sweet apple scent of chamomile flowers is like salve to the psyche, the tender flowers like little magic suns, their bright yellow centers framed by tiny, white, velvety petals sitting on a spray of green foliage fine as lace doilies. Pollinating bees tiptoe across the golden florets with sticky legs and sweet intentions.

The combination of chamomile flowers, fennel seeds, and fresh lemon peel is a digestive recipe dating back over generations of matron saints in Rome. It harkens back to a time when a kindly Italian grandmother would serve this blend to her friends and family after a satisfying meal of gnocchi, fava beans, pecorino, and ample amounts of Nebbiolo red wine.

In the traditional formula, boiling spring water is poured over the trinity of flavors and raw amber-hued honey is drizzled into the nectar. Fresh lemon zest is grated into the final elixir for a sparkling, life-affirming top note.

While the medicinal use of chamomile alleviates anxiety and calms worries, the Gypsies believe it brings luck and money to those who bathe in it. "Allow the scent of fortune to soak deeply into your skin." I believe in the magic of chamomile. It's played an essential role in healing serums since prehistoric times, cooling inflammation of the body and mind. Press the flowers in your wallet to attract wealth, and after washing your hands in it you will win at gambling.

My father raised me to be fiercely independent. His mantras were, "You are your work. Depend on no one"; "Hard work is honest work"; and "Don't be a deadbeat. Make your own way." As a result, after Sage was born, I wasn't eager to let anyone know how badly my first run at motherhood was turning out. My storybook ideal was simple: (1) home birth with a kind midwife to fuss over me, and (2) stay-at-home career as a writer that would allow me to be there for every moment of Sage's childhood. My perfect plan shattered when my relationship crumbled, my writing stalled, and my baby had to be born in a hospital due to complications. And now my perfect boy had special needs.

When I returned from the hospital with six-week-old Sage in my arms, I felt like the biggest failure on the planet. I had no idea how I was going to rebuild my life, but I knew one thing for sure—I was going to do it on my own. I was a big girl and knew where my bootstraps were located.

Sage slept peacefully, as if those first weeks of crying and discomfort had never happened. He was a beam of light. I learned to carefully maneuver around the tubes that ran in and out of his abdomen and diaper, but I lost sleep to worry and an endless, debilitating migraine. I was drained of spirit by the pressure and doubt. If I made a mistake with Sage's care, it could be life and death. The knowledge that he could so easily be taken from me by the slightest infection pushed my psyche to the edge. I felt as if God had picked the wrong mom.

Dark circles under my eyes deepened to purple, giving me that authentic zombie look. I held Sage and stared out the window for hours. No inspiration dawned. No answers arrived. And while I rocked between "How did I get here?" and "What do I do now?" no food magically appeared in the refrigerator. I was a hot mess in need of a hot meal, and my bootstraps were decidedly out of reach.

The pediatric urologist had said breast milk was the best thing for Sage's kidneys. If I didn't eat, he didn't eat. I would happily have starved rather than let anyone see me in this sad state, but pride wasn't going to feed this baby. It was time to reexamine my Dad-given hang-ups around "handouts."

I considered my options. Call my parents? No way. Call my high school best friend? She was struggling herself. I had built a fortress around myself, a fortress of *I. I* am strong. I am self-sufficient. I am independent of you—whoever you are. But now I was no longer one person, alone. *I* was now *we.*

My neighbor came to mind. Every time I saw her she radiated a soothing energy, always moving around her garden with a sweet grace. She and I weren't yet friends, but I felt that maybe I could ask for some citrus from her trees, or some of the butternut squash that grew over the ledge of her garden into my yard.

I strategized for hours about how to get some of those delicious-looking veggies on my stove. I'd play it cool, I thought. I could make it casual, like, "Hey, I'd love to try some of those zucchini. How about we trade—my herbal teas for your veggies?"

Finally, with great trepidation, I picked up the phone and dialed her number, the one she'd shared in case of emergency—our canyon was prone to floods and fires. And it was pouring outside.

"Hello," she answered.

"Hi, Ava, it's your neighbor, Zhena."

"Oh, hi, honey, how are you? How is the baby?"

"Fine. Well, actually, um, not so fine really." My throat tried to clamp down on the confession, but I plowed through.

"What's going on?" she asked.

"Well, he almost had kidney failure. We thought it was colic." Tears burned my eyes. Crap. I hadn't planned on telling her the truth.

"Oh, my God, I am so sorry. Are you okay? How is he?"

Now the words rushed out. "I think he's going to be okay. He has a hole they made in his bladder and sewed it to the outside of his tummy so the urine will drain and not build up and make his kidneys nephritic, or swollen." Although I was terrified to say this, it gave my heart a reprieve. Having this new reality was one thing, but saying it, claiming it out loud, somehow started the healing process for me.

"Poor little Sage," she said. "Can I bring you anything?"

"Um"—I looked down at Sage—"yes, actually, I'm really hungry and nursing and can't make anything from what's here." There. It was done.

She didn't hesitate. "Give me an hour."

And that was it. My face burned with embarrassment, I felt a tightness in my solar plexus, and my hands shook as I hung up, but I had broken this senseless self-reliant streak wide open and I felt . . . hopeful. The haze of sadness and fear was receding, and on the immediate horizon, sailing toward me, were compassion, food, and friendship.

Keeping a distance from others had been a prominent part of my Ukrainian upbringing. When I was young, my grandma Maria often baked loaves of bread for her entire congregation, which took her all week. Her generosity was a sort of ongoing payment to others for allowing her to be in their lives. She baked until the flour and eggs were gone and she was spent, sipping tea on her chair, breathing hard, and totally fulfilled by her giving. But when she needed to be prayed for, when the doctor discovered stage-4 cancer throughout her entire body, she forbade any of us to tell her congregation, because she didn't want to "be a bother" to them. She taught us to "never put anyone out," to be the least expensive person in the room, and that selflessness was its own reward.

Now I realized this mentality made it impossible to be truly close to anyone, unless I was need-free. Never wanting to be "a bother" had made it easy to be social, but it had also isolated me. Asking for help was a bridge I hadn't ventured over before, and I felt shaky in the new intimacy I would now have with my neighbor. I wondered how many times I had shut out someone who wished to contribute in some way to my life. Even when broke, I never let a friend pick up the bill, even if it meant going into overdraft.

Shame returned to my mind, with a lot of other baggage. Back in our Ukrainian village, one of my great-great uncles was the village "strong man." And during my childhood in California, my firefighter father was a role model of toughness. I remembered when Dad had fallen from a tree, breaking his leg in half, only to use a log and some rope to reset it so he could show up to his weekday job at the US Forest Service to grade fire roads. Once he cut his arm to the bone on a rusty wood splitter blade, sealed it with a T-shirt and electrical tape, and went about cutting a nice cord of oak for our neighbor. I had begged him to go to the doctor, crying as I imagined a fever coming to take him away like it had to a character on *Little House on the Prairie*. He shrugged me off. He was bitten by a scorpion while fighting the cave fires in Santa Barbara but kept quiet about it so he wouldn't get sent home and lose the hazard pay—so us kids could have a "good Christmas." After a long day out in the forest, cutting down trees for extra cash, he drove the windy Jalama Ranch Road, dodged a deer while taking a corner, and rolled his truck over a cliff, only to show up casually in the kitchen with his head duct-taped together and a frosty Coors Light in hand. Leaning on the fridge, he asked Mom what was for dinner. Keeping it together, remaining the provider during feats of total awesomeness, was his MO.

Maybe these generations of tough men had transformed our DNA so that showing weakness and asking for help was humiliating. As I waited for my neighbor, I almost called her to say, "Never mind, it's all good," just to keep my dignity intact.

Before I could cancel, Ava knocked at the front door and let herself in. Dripping wet in her yellow poncho, a massive pot of lentil soup on her hip and a mason jar full of golden liquid under her arm, she smiled at me, went right to the stove, and lit the pilot.

The smell of herbs filled the cabin as she poured the contents of the canning jar into a cup.

She said, "This is an old recipe from Rome, from my grandmother. It's chamomile, fennel seeds, and lemon peel. It'll calm you, help your milk come in, and keep the baby from getting gas. The the lemon is just for flavor—oh, and I guess a little optimism."

I took the cup and smiled up at her, speechless.

"The soup will feed you for a week," she said. "I'll bring you veggies so you can keep adding to it."

I inhaled the tea's sweet aroma—apples and licorice. I sipped and the heat warmed my chest. As the rain pounded on the metal roof, I felt a sun rising in me. Sage woke up, and I sat with him in my arms.

And then she sat next to me and listened to my story. The whole thing.

When Fear of Showing Weakness Is the Greatest Weakness of All

Mantra of the Cup: My weaknesses open the door to my undiscovered strengths. I ask and receive all that I need with ease and clarity.

I was recently in a room full of fifty female executives from Fortune 100 companies, international banks, the US and Canadian governments, and MBA professors. I asked the audience of brilliant women at the top of their game to raise their hands if they had a hard time asking for help—and all but two did.

Not asking for help makes us feel like we are in control, even when we're not. We find comfort in believing we are in charge. When we are giving, we are in control, and when we are receiving, we aren't. I was used to giving, controlling, managing, being the village "strong woman" in my own life, but when it came to Sage, I went through a spiritual shakedown.

This is how fellowship is born. We eventually realize that muscling solo through a problem gives us only the illusion of control. But when we learn to ask for help, we allow others to participate in our life and invest in the relationship. While we may feel that we are asking "too much" in asking for assistance, people generally feel honored by our sincerity and our admission of vulnerability. We give them a gift by allowing them to help.

The price of holding on to pride is so much higher than the cost of giving it up. Being strong, independent, and contribution-minded is great, except in those times when you simply need a hug, a warm meal, or a compassionate act of kindness. Even when you are crying in a heap, you are worthy of grace, love, and goodwill.

The key to asking for help and receiving it is to make it a practice, a discipline, rather than a symbolic albatross around your neck. Asking is not shameful; it's not wrong. We often don't do it because we haven't learned it's okay. We aren't taught how to ask. When we need help most is often when our fear of showing weakness is our weakness. Making specific, step-by-step requests is a great way to shift from going it alone to accepting fellowship from others. Allow yourself to take the helping hand that others are just waiting to extend to you.

Exercise: Make a Specific Request

Are you a sparkling specific, or a wandering generality?

—ZIG ZIGLAR

In this exercise, you'll flex your asking-and-receiving muscles by making a specific request of someone. Whether or not the person you ask for help says yes doesn't matter so much. What does matter is that you will have succeeded in mustering the courage to show your vulnerability and to do something about it.

The trick to asking for help is to be specific in your request. Perhaps you need something from your mate, boss, client, friend, teacher, neighbor, parent, or sibling. You can make it easy for others to say yes when you are specific, because other people can honestly assess whether or not they can help you. A general cry for help might be all you can bear, and that's okay, but by defining your request you have to examine your needs. Even if the first person you ask has to say no, you've kept your dignity.

What do you really need in your life, today, but are afraid or hesitant to ask for? Is it a hug, help with household tasks, some advice, money, more attention from your mate or recognition from your boss? Imagine yourself asking for whatever it is with a genuinely open heart, without attachment to their answer. Generate that courage; here we go.

1. Identify something specific that you really want and need.

2. Identify whom you need it from.

3. Set a time with the person to call or meet—give yourself a deadline.

4. Write out a specific request as rehearsal for your talk or meeting. You are not going to email or mail this request. You're writing it down to engage your mind and body into following through on your request.

> Dear _____,
>
> I'm grateful/thankful to have you in my life.
> I have a request for you: _____.
> I appreciate your willingness to help me. Please let me
>   know if you can help by _____.
>
> Thank you.

5. The elements of your request are the person whom you're asking for help, a phrase of gratitude, what exactly you need (if it's "more love," you need to be specific about what form it should take, such as more touching or encouragement, or whatever your "love language" might be), a date you need help by, and gratitude for the person's willingness to consider your request.

6. Writing out your request makes it easier for you to stay on track when you do meet the person and ask. It keeps your request succinct, helps you manage your emotions, and lets you stay focused on being specific. Keep your written request on hand to refer to if your mind goes blank once you are live with the other person.

7. After you ask, do your best to then be quiet long enough for them to respond. Resist the urge to talk away your discomfort. Give the other person time to process your request and answer you. The answer may surprise you— you may get an unconditional yes or you may get a no with an offer to help you in a different way that is even more helpful then a yes!

Ask and it shall be given you.

—MATTHEW 7:7

3

Just Show Up

A Cup of Lavender Blossoms and Local Heroes

*Intuition is a spiritual faculty and does not explain,
but simply points the way.*

—FLORENCE SCOVEL SHINN

Inspiration: The gentle strength of lavender. Lavender grows like purple wildfire in the Ojai Valley but is native to the Mediterranean, Africa, and India. After Sage was born, I would go to the local farmers' market to inhale the soothing scent of lavender from the bouquets the growers had brought to sell. Although I couldn't afford to buy any of their perfectly cut, ribbon-tied arrangements, they gave me cuttings to plant along the edge of my cabin. When the flowers bloomed, I clipped and blended them into a tea with a ruby-red bark called Rooibos from South Africa. I drank this tea to stay calm and also enjoyed the unexpected side effects that include positive thoughts, a spiritual focus, and an unraveling of my tightly wound nerves. I would roll the downy lavender flowers in my hands and inhale my palms. Its relaxing scent gave me a quiet courage and inspiration. The reddish-purple liqueur helped me dream of a better life for my son and me, as I worked two days a week at a boutique selling wealthy tourists expensive shoes and clothes.

Rooibos is traditionally used by mothers throughout Africa to treat colic in their babies, as it eases tummy troubles. Its ruby-hued liqueur also enhances collagen, making it a time-tested beautifier. Its bark is soft and shiny, and when cut and sifted it looks like little red needles poking through tea-bag paper. Rooibos allays doubt and uncertainty. It infuses our cells with trace minerals absorbed from the rich Cederberg Mountain range soil in South Africa, where it grows over seven feet high and leans in the wind, reaching for the sun.

One day, during my lunch break, I noticed that the café-bookstore, which had long been part of the Ojai community, had a For Sale sign on it. A framed, carefully lettered notice said, AFTER MANY SEASONS OF SUCCESS AND JOY, WE HAVE DECIDED TO SELL. IF YOU ARE INTERESTED, PLEASE CONTACT OWNER.

"Hmmm," I thought.

Now, I was in no position to buy a café-bookstore, but something in me sparked at the thought. I envisioned reading to a group of children in the zebra-carpeted kids' section and afternoons of Gypsy violins playing in the courtyard, the lingering scent of fresh oolong tea mingling in the air with rapturous songs. Twinkling sounds of laughter and applause would travel though the garden doors as I added up the daily sales with a smile on my face.

Back at the boutique, I was actually shaking from the vision of running my own bookstore-teahouse. I sneaked into the back office and eyeballed the phone. What if I just called to ask? I could make up a name so the owner wouldn't know it was just that shopgirl with the frizzy hair and loud laugh. Before I had the chance to embarrass myself, I went back into the store and busied myself rearranging a round rack of knit twinsets.

All that day, I trembled a little with a delicious sort of delight. I had a sense of "Reach for this and you will meet your peril!"—but in an invigorating way. At the end of my shift, I went back in the owner's office. The phone seemed to pulse and glow under the little Tiffany lamp on my boss's desk. I so badly wanted to reach for it, but once again, sanity prevailed.

Although I didn't think it was my end-all destiny to sell clothes and shoes, I did love working there and didn't want to risk losing my job. Things were working out: My family took turns watching Sage while I earned enough to cover gas to and from work, a lunchtime veggie burrito, and diapers. After paying the monthly basics, I could make a small payment to the hospital. Paying $35 a month on a $17,000 bill felt like chipping away at Mount Everest with a pair of tweezers, but it made me hopeful I could gain a footing. It didn't make sense to throw away the little bit of security I had in favor of a high-falutin' fantasy.

I started envisioning the negative side of making that call: Surely the bookstore owner would find my hubris outrageous. Soon everyone in town would know of my foolishness and come into the dress shop just to laugh at me. I would be fired. The collection agents would set up a tent city on my lawn. My parents would burn my baby pictures. I'd get evicted. Sage and I would be reduced to living in my car and begging for croutons outside Carrows.

But no amount of catastrophic thinking quelled my excitement. I buzzed all night with visions of a Gypsy Tearoom with my grandmother's beautiful, hand-embroidered tapestries hanging on the walls, a selection of elegant teas and freshly roasted coffee, and an international newsstand so everyone in our small town could feel the vastness of the universe while sipping, browsing, and buying books.

I set up an appointment to meet with the owner. I had no idea what I was doing, but I had two weeks to figure it out.

I called my friend Gaston, a world-class restaurateur, entrepreneur, and musician who lives in Carmel-by-the-Sea, and asked for advice. He asked if people would drink hot tea in Ojai when our summer temperatures are in the hundreds. I assured him that iced tea and chilled champagne, beer, and coffee drinks would fill in the revenue gaps.

As I was talking, I suddenly realized that I was actually smart in something. It was like my intellect had caught fire and I innately knew what to do and how to do it. I asked Gaston if this was okay or even normal, and he said, "When you find what you are passionate about, my bets are on you." It was the encouragement I needed, coming from someone I admired.

While Sage napped, I wrote a business plan, researched tea importers, and designed a remodel for the patio, adding fountains, a large shade structure, and tiles designed by local artists. I was moving so fast that fear couldn't catch me.

The day of the meeting I donned my one suit, dressed it up

with some funky Gypsy jewelry, put my hair back, climbed into some very high heels, and teetered out the door to meet my bright future. Then I saw my car as if for the first time. Three shades of gray, including the panels that were coated in primer. Some feral cats had taken the lack of a driver's side window as an invitation to have a mating party in there. They had clawed the driver's seat, releasing particles of clingy, yellow foam so tiny that I inhaled some and couldn't stop sneezing.

I ran back to the house, found a towel to cover the seat, and started the car, frightening a squirrel out of the wheel well. I was off, my carefully printed business plan in the folder next to me.

As I drove the ten miles from my cabin to town, I started to get really nervous. Throw-up nervous. It was a sensation first, and then an emotion, then a voice in my head said, "What the hell do you think you are doing?"

I kept driving, and the voice got louder, "Who do you think you are? You have no money, no experience, no backers, no husband to cover the bills, no anything but a baby who needs you to be there for him."

I slowed down and pulled to the side of the road, next to the river, which flowed loudly from the winter rains. I looked around at the trees and the mountains. I looked at myself in the rearview mirror, staring hard into my own eyes for a while.

Another voice piped in, "Just show up."

"Right," I argued, "just show up in my beater car and thrift store suit like a complete loser."

"*Just show up*," the voice insisted. This voice wasn't hysteria-tinged like the critical one.

So I pulled back onto the road, toward town.

"What do I say when he asks me about capital?"

"JUST SHOW UP."

"What if he checks my credit?"

"JUST SHOW UP."

"Why would he finance me when I'm so broke?"

"JUST SHOW UP."

This voice was settled and sure, so I obeyed it.

I parked about six blocks away and picked my way over the stone streets toward the bookstore. Two doors down, I thought to run into the little department store and take a look in the mirror one last time. The owner was a Hollywood guy and was probably used to really polished looks.

In the dressing room I smoothed the suit coat—not too bad. It was a vintage three-piece of thinly spun wool, low cut enough to show a bit of lace camisole. I felt powerful in it. I was nursing Sage at the time so my chest filled out the jacket. I reapplied mascara, blush, and lipstick and decided to take my hair down. As I shook out my hair, I caught a glimpse of my backside and gasped. Milky white baby spit-up crusted the back of the coat and my butt. The towel I'd put on the seat! I had grabbed it out of the laundry basket.

Breaking for the bathroom, I wet paper towels in the sink and scrubbed at the gunk, the paper towels disintegrating and making double trouble for my suit.

"See, you fool? You are not up to this!"

I kept scrubbing.

"Thinking you're so hot. This is a sign! Turn back now and no one will be the wiser!"

I stopped scrubbing. The voice was right. I didn't have any money, just some good ideas. I needed to accept where I was and go home.

But then I caught my eyes in the mirror. They weren't filled with fear. They were rock steady. I heard, clear and ringing, "JUST SHOW UP." I turned around, and walked right into the bookstore.

The owner was a filmmaker and producer who loved the café, but he had been supporting it with other income.

"I've tried everything I can think of to get revenues up," he confided.

It was like he was so in the day-to-day he couldn't see the potential that I had seen. I asked him every question that Gaston had coached me on, about lease structure and building maintenance, and I wasn't self-conscious for one second. I showed him the revenue projections, my ideas for merchandising, the change in the floor plan, and my new menu ideas. We bounced ideas back and forth and the energy was bright and shiny between us. For every idea I had, he got more excited, and before long, hours had passed and it was time for me to get home to Sage.

I said, "So, will you finance the business for me, now that you know what I'm going to make of it?"

"Why would I do that? Why would I sell it, just to have it become so much better—even though I'll still be financing it? Why wouldn't I just hire you as a consultant and pay you to do it for me?"

"Oh. Well, because I need a place where I can have my son with me. He has a condition and I thought if I owned it, I could bring him to work."

He replied, "Bring him. Just get these things done as your plan shows and it will be all good."

Just Show Up

Mantra of the Cup: I show up to my greatness every day.

I met a woman who was a major hedge fund sales executive in New York City. She built her career from the ground up, transforming herself from an analyst to the top sales producer of her asset management company. As a bona-fide superstar in her field, she would listen to the "money" people talk in jargon that intimidated regular folk and make them feel small, insignificant, and confused. She jumped ship in order to start her own website that would demystify the money language by making it fun and funny for those outside her industry—regular people like you and me (assuming you don't run a hedge fund, of course). Her desire is to do for money what Jon Stewart does for news—make it educational and funny and therefore empowering. I asked her what her revenue model would be for the site, and she flashed her beautiful hazel eyes and said, "I don't know, I'm figuring it out as I go."

She's "just showing up."

She said everybody thinks she's lost her mind. Even her hairdresser panicked when he learned she'd given up her huge salary to start a website to make money funny. Friends have vanished, shaking their heads in worry. Former colleagues think she's crazy, but she's showing up every day for her vision anyway.

By showing up you are taking an action, and actions are what bring results, whether or not you are competent yet in something, A thousand ideas come and go in our minds, but the ones we actually make a move toward are the ones that pay off, even if we don't know exactly how to get it done.

What you show up for shows who you are. If you want to be

a writer, you have to show up at the computer even if you have no idea what you will write. Start writing and it begins to form. If you want to own a business, even with no resources to your name, getting the business plan written takes no money—only effort—but it's proof of your willingness to show up to owning a business. If you want to be married, you've got to show up for yourself—the way a potential mate would, with kindness and care.

Showing up doesn't take a lot of brains; it doesn't take an MBA or a PhD; it doesn't take perfect grammar or a loaded bank account. The best stories of great businesses have simple beginnings. Mrs. Fields started baking cookies in her kitchen; Steve Jobs started Apple in a garage, and Estée Lauder made lotion in her bathtub. These entrepreneurs just kept showing up day after day, baking cookies, building computers, and mixing potions. These fun stories of the early years of businesses, when the founders had no idea if they would work but were exhilarated by the work itself, give us permission to show up, too, maybe with nothing but a willingness to look like a fool for a dream.

You do not need to wait until all is perfect to start moving in the direction of your dream. When you take the leap to show up, you build your confidence and self-esteem. Showing up demands that you quiet the voices in your head or the criticism from family and friends so that you can rise to the task at hand. Actions are proof of your commitment. What you show up for makes your commitment evident in your external world, which enables the world to react to you so that you can learn and move forward. Your actions and commitments are the only things that are real when it comes to achieving results—your internal doubts are not real.

Showing up takes guts, especially when your doubts are carrying a big stick and coming right at you.

Exercise: Show Up for Your Dreams

The stronger you allow your dream to get, the easier it is to show up for it. The more you define your intention, the more empowered you become. Knowing what you don't want is key to knowing what you do want, so in this exercise you will define what you want, which will help you show up for it. Even in the act of identifying your dream, you are showing up for it. So brew your cup of tea and get out a pen and paper. Defining your dream gives you a destination.

1. Identify your big dreams (ex: to have a baby, to start a business, or to take your mom to Italy). Write down one big dream.

2. If you cannot identify a single dream, then think about something that has been quietly nagging at you. It could be to make more money, start painting, win an award, or be a leader in your field. Whatever it is, write it on the top of the paper or define it clearly in your mind's eye.

3. Phrase your dream with positive words. For example, I want to lose ten pounds turns into I want a healthy, more svelte body that weighs _____ pounds. I want to start and grow a business that allows my family and me to travel. I want to make plenty of money by helping the causes that matter most to me. When you phrase your dream in the positive, your subconscious mind is more likely to achieve it.

4. Write five things you can do TODAY to show up for that dream. For example, if your dream is to make more

money at your company, you could write, I will confidently wear my best suit/dress/shoes/shirt to work; I will show up early; I will set a meeting with my boss and make a specific request for more responsibilities in exchange for more money; I will organize my schedule efficiently to follow through on my commitment.

5. Keep eye contact with your vision/dream daily. Write it and post it where you can see it. Put it everywhere—in your car, on your bathroom mirror, the refrigerator door, the case of your smartphone, and as your screen saver. Do five things a day to move yourself toward your dream. Remember, you're building evidence and showing your commitment to your vision by doing this. Even if you don't know how you'll get there, your actions will magically carry you toward it.

Faith is taking the first step, even when you don't see
the whole staircase.

—MARTIN LUTHER KING JR.

The intellect has little to do on the road to discovery.
There comes a leap in consciousness, call it intuition
or what you will, and the solution comes to you
and you don't know how or why.

—ALBERT EINSTEIN

4

Start Where You Are

A Cup of Milk and Honey

Do not wait to strike till the iron is hot;
but make it hot by striking.

—WILLIAM BUTLER YEATS

Inspiration: Creamy sweet tea lattes with steamed milk, warm golden honey, fresh muddled herbs from a sunshine-soaked California desert garden, and a sprinkle of resourcefulness. Black teas work best for lattes. I pulverize full leaves in a coffee grinder reserved for spices in order to get the strongest steep and most balanced tannins. Then I soak the tea in freshly steamed milk until the bright white foam turns a burnt-sugar brown. I strain the leaves from the milk through a sterling silver strainer with jade in the handle, which adds magic to the ritual. Magic is an ingredient you can feel but not always taste.

Working at the bookstore-café, I was able to play with the equipment as if I were in my very own lab, while Sage cooed and gurgled in his sling. I ordered a lot of free samples of teas from suppliers the world over. With boxes of teas and culinary spices, and some simple syrups, I went about curating rare teas, combining them with aromatic spices and medicinal herbs, and I designed a tea menu with my very own unique beverages. My tea lattes paired creamy caramel with a sprinkle of pink Himalayan salt, heady French vanilla with freshly plucked crimson rose petals, and earthy hazelnut with hand-ground Vietnamese cinnamon. I created a menu of exotic, palate-teasing journeys that took me to every corner of the world I'd wanted to visit.

Dreaming up blends was so pleasurable, the energy of creation so delicious. I ground cardamom pods in my mortar and added rosemary with white tea for a mystical Turkish afternoon elixir for royalty. I steeped fresh star jasmine blossoms and Chinese spring Dragon Well green tea leaves in homemade almond milk with fresh orange blossom honey. I simmered fleshy pink rose petals with heady Egyptian Mint syrup and young green tea buds. In this creative space, unexpected flavor marriages occurred, like apricot and garam masala, turmeric and sunflower, violet and white chocolate. I toiled away in bliss, spicing the blends with melted turbinado sugar syrups, soul-nourishing tinctures, and piquant herbs from my garden.

For six months, I poured all of my passion into these formulations, pairing ingredients by color, scent, and energy. I began pining to have my own teahouse, the one I'd first envisioned when I'd seen that For Sale sign at the bookstore. Now that I had food on the table, I could relax a little, but the desire for my own business was growing. The more creative I got, the more I craved ownership of my time and efforts. From a particle of sand in my imagination, a pearl had started to form.

Each of us is born with a particular genius, a kernel of talent that lies latent until we root it out and bring it into the light to be shared. Our job in life, our purpose, is to uncover and use it. Every experience is a chance to get a step closer to it. When we've tapped into this gift, we become enthusiastic, energized, and electric. Our life sparkles with hope and excitement. I believe I tapped into my genius by making these "potions" of blended teas. The practice was life-affirming. It engaged all of my senses and made time feel expansive.

I had studied herbs, traveled to Peru with ethnobotanists pursuing indigenous medicinal use of rain forest herbs, taken aromatherapy classes, and often dreamed of becoming a perfumer. I cherished plants and the power they held in their volatile oils. Unlocking the scent of a leaf, flower, pod, or stem felt as if I were unleashing the secrets of the universe. When I was formulating a new blend, there were no worries, no poverty, no bills, no fear of the future, nothing but love. I felt integrated—in my *integrity*.

Our cells hold within them the memory of our ancestors, and I had several medicine women in my lineage. In family mythology, my great-great-grandmother on my mother's side was a blue-eyed medicine woman from Arizona territory, while my great-great grandmother on my father's side was a traveling healer with the Moscow circus. Perhaps these influences conspired to make me a "potion maker."

Just as perfume can enhance a mood, inspire love, and spice up or calm a moment in life, I was convinced tea could do these things, too. So I used the perfumer methodology of combining a base note, mid note, and high note to blend my teas. We can taste combinations of essential oils by inhaling their aroma, so I mixed drops of oils into tea leaves to carry their scents onto our palates. I imagined right into the heart and soul of people who would sip my concoctions.

My motto is: A tea for all the senses. I tested and formulated each tea to appeal to sight, smell, sound, touch and taste.

See: The tea should be colorful and attract the eye.

Smell: The blend should have a perfect balance of notes and be as addictive as a signature scent is.

Hear: The tea should have a beautiful story to it, one that could inspire your imagination each time you had a cup.

Touch: The loose leaves should be fun to touch and should increase your curiosity.

Taste: All of the elements of balance, flavor, and experiential bliss should land and dance on the tongue.

Each layer of each blend should be meaningful, each tea experience a ritual in mindfulness that helps the tea drinker to expand more fully into her body through her senses. My blends aim to communicate with the whole person, because the base, mid, and high notes of the scents correspond to the body, heart, and mind.

I shopped my business idea for a Gypsy Tearoom to my friends and family, and they generously loaned me about $3,000. It was nowhere near the $150,000 the business plan called for, but it still seemed like so much money to me. I thought that, surely, I could get *something* going with it.

Three thousand could get me a couple months' rent of a storefront in Ojai's shopping plaza, or it could build a website to sell tea online—but either would use up my seed money before I could build a customer base. Before I had a chance to talk myself down from the dream, return the money to my investors, and settle for the safety of a regular paycheck, I stumbled upon a hip consignment store in the neighboring town of Ventura in a sun-filled renovated warehouse. The décor and merchandise were so chic that, although I couldn't afford to buy anything, I kept browsing just to be in the space.

As Sage dozed in his baby carrier, I struck up a conversation with the two women behind the counter, who were the owners.

"I want to start my own business," I said, "but only if I can create the kind of perfection you've got here."

They lit up as I told them about my Gypsy Tearoom. I explained the perfumed scents of the exotic tea leaves, described my method of blending and creating creamy tea lattes, and shared how each tea had transporting flavors and aromatherapy for enhancing mood. They finally said, "Bring it here!" They were so enthusiastic. Within moments we'd all agreed that I'd pay 10 percent of my sales for rent. No big lease agreements, no credit checks, only a meeting of like minds. I'd just taken the next step toward my dream.

Starting small was better than not starting at all. I sowed that seed money from my parents, my little brothers, and my childhood best friend with love and care. They had given me their hard-earned money, even though they didn't have excess. Each dollar came from their hard work, and by investing in my idea, they'd shown their belief in me. Their goodwill was a powerful force, and their hope made me determined to make it work.

With a friend's help, I found a used espresso cart made from mahogany laminate and black lacquer with touches of brass, shined it up, and opened the side counters to make it bigger. It reminded me of Gypsy wagons in my grandmother's caravan. It was perfect. It was beautiful. Then I collected chairs and bistro tables from thrift stores, including a yellow slipcovered couch and a low coffee table made from a hand-carved southern Indian door. A café down the street lost its lease and sold off every item a teahouse could want for mere pennies on the dollar. I outfitted my makeshift café for under $3,000, and when I stood back to look at it, a business owner's pride rose in me. It was my love made evident.

On opening day I drove out of the canyon at 7:05 a.m. as a business *owner*! I felt like a rock star! Wait, I *was* a rock star! I imagined the crowds, the line out the door to taste my unusual tea concoctions! I saw the surprised and satisfied smiles mustached with latte foam. They'd rush the cart to get seconds, throwing money at the till to get more!

Sage smiled at me from his car seat.

"Just a quick stop at the bank, little man, so we can get milk to make the tea lattes on my *real* menu board."

I grinned as we sputtered up to the ATM. I didn't care that my car was ugly, because *I was a business owner.* I was queen of the world!

My grin faltered when I saw that my balance was only $6. I scratched my head. Who came up with the rule that ATMs only dispense twenties? No milk, no tea lattes. I yanked on the doors. The bank wasn't open yet.

I was so used to running on empty that instead of worrying about how little money I had, I worried about how to get it out of the bank's clutches in order to spend it on milk and honey. I had to get the tea cart up and running. It was opening day!

At the store, I set a gallon of organic milk and a small [
bear on the counter, handed over my debit card, and hel[
breath. Transaction complete! My balance was now just ov[
dollar. After I put him back into his car seat, I held Sage's per[
little face in my hands and said, "This better work."

I had spent the night before hand-making tea bags. I'd blend[
loose-leaf tea in a big silver bowl, poured it into corsage bag[
tucked in a Gypsy "fortune," and then tied each up with a bow[
The fortunes were quotes from Grandma Maria: "Do not leave [
caravan midjourney," "Don't sit on a fence. Be passionate about[
SOMETHING!" I loved the chance to channel her distinctive,
comforting energy.

Sage was irresistible in his green corduroy coveralls, the first
wisps of his hair shone a shimmering red, and his big green eyes
sparkled. There was no way anyone would know that he had un-
dergone such a huge operation a few months earlier. He smiled
and clapped his hands, inspiring me to keep moving in the direction of my dream. We were a unit and we were out to sell some
tea lattes!

At the shop, the owners had put little vases of fresh flowers on
the bistro tables. The owners were all hugs and encouragement.
I strapped Sage into the baby sling and went about prepping the
cart. I put the milk in the fridge, set out the little honey bear, and
displayed the scones I'd baked. The corsage bags of tea looked like
a tray of jewels. I polished the espresso maker. I fluffed the pillows
on the yellow couch. At 9 o'clock, when the owners opened the
doors, I was on fire to serve my public.

I peeked outside and there was no line out the door. I figured
maybe people just didn't know I was there yet, so I handwrote
some signs and posted them on the windows. I waited, perplexed

ners of the shop bought three lattes apiece
ay one: $18.

ed marketing, and the next day, I walked up
with a tray of samples. I popped into the salons
ng out little tastes of Vanilla Rose tea latte. The
door told their clients, and within hours, a few
women appeared at my cart and ordered my teas.

I did the same with the Hazelnut Cinnamon black
ing all the stores within five blocks. Sage rode high
baby backpack, hitting me on the head as I told the
about the secret tea oasis just a few doors down. By the
e week, I was averaging $40 a day. Not earth-shattering,
bank balance was now high enough that I could with-
fat $20 if I needed it. I had gone from making $10 an hour
ing for someone else to making $7.50 working for myself. It
n't going to get me to the $150,000 I needed to open my own
psy Tearoom anytime soon, but it was a pay cut that got me
ne step closer to my destiny.

Start Where You Are

*Mantra of the Cup: Today, right now, I have everything
I need to uncover my genius and start making it
more evident in the world.*

What is your unique form of genius and how can you start
making it more evident in the world . . . today? Whatever your
dream, the key is to get going on making it real no matter your
current circumstances. The universe rewards those who act on
their genius!

I met a breathtakingly beautiful former model who wanted to open her own tea spa. Fit and focused, she was an ideal spa spokeswoman who looked and lived the part. I was excited for her and we spent a lot of time together tasting teas and dreaming up tea beauty treatments. For months she researched tea supplies and worked on her plan, perfecting her concept and designing the perfect consumer experience. But she just kept doing that, over and over, and eventually she analyzed herself out of ever actually starting her business. She had a vision in her mind that was ideal, but she couldn't bring herself to start. She never believed there was enough time or money or the right lease in her city. Reality looked way too different from her vision, and she got discouraged and quit.

Working to achieve perfect conditions can stop you from taking the one defining step toward your dream. The first step is rarely as perfect as it is in your mind's eye, but one foot forward takes you toward it. The biggest loss is when you don't push past the resistance to begin. Starting and stepping up build evidence of your dreams in the world outside your mind. As the evidence builds, your confidence grows and your steps gain momentum.

Break up long-term goals into daily steps and your destiny will reveal itself a little more with each one. Start to build evidence that your dream is real in the world. Your reward will be that you get what you want. It might not be exactly how you envisioned it, but it will be perfect because it will be real.

Starting today means pushing past the current situation to get into the ideal one—one tiny step at a time. Think of it as working in sips. Life is so much more manageable in sips. Imagine that your destiny is written by angels and it lies at the bottom of your cup, just waiting for you to drink the tea to reveal it. There are only two rules: (1) You cannot pour out the tea all at once to see it, and (2) You have to enjoy the tea, you have to *sip* it, and taste it, slowly reaching the message hidden beneath it.

That's how showing up works. You don't know exactly how you'll get to your destination, but you really will be happier if you enjoy the journey, one tiny sip at a time.

There's a saying that a pickpocket sees only pockets. Meaning you get what you look for. If you look for your genius, you'll find it. If you look for a way to express your genius, you'll discover the path. On the flip side, if you look for failure, then that's what you'll get. If you look for all the reasons why something can't work, then that's all you'll see. When you decide to make something happen, to start something that will matter to you and the world, you redefine the possible. Even if you don't have all the resources at your fingertips, you have to make that leap. Resourcefulness is born of starting today.

Now imagine looking back in a year on this very day: How would it feel if you didn't take action toward your dream? What will you most regret—starting or not starting?

Exercise: Starting Where You Are

Today is the day that matters most. It might feel like just another one for the records, but it promises So. Much. More! Taking the first step toward your dreams is the scariest but it is also the most empowering. You may feel nervous, incapable, and doubtful. Worry may take hold of you and shake your resolve, but somewhere in your soul you have the insight that your life can be brighter and bigger somehow. Whenever an intuition or a dream takes hold of your thoughts, the next step is to build evidence of it in the world.

Write out where you are today and where you want to be in a year (or six months) in the following categories (or pick which ones you want to work on):

1. Love
2. Money
3. Work
4. Family
5. Friends
6. Body
7. Mind
8. Spirit

Where you are now: Write this in a notebook or journal or the note section on your smartphone.

1. Love: I am _____ (ex: married, single, dating).
2. Money: My assets are worth _____ (dollar amount).
3. Work: I am working at _____ (ex: a part-time/full-time job, a business of my own, looking for work).
4. Family: I am in a family of _____ (number).
5. Friends: I have lots of acquaintances and _____ (number) close friends.
6. Body: I am in _____ shape. I weigh _____.
7. Mind: I am knowledgeable in _____ and competent in _____.
8. Spirit: I believe in _____. I practice my faith by _____.

Now write where you want to be in your ideal situation in each area of your life, but write in the present tense. As you write, visualize your answers and feel them happening for you. What does it feel like in your body to be in the ideal state in each category?

1. My love is fulfilling because ____. My relationship makes my life better because ____.

2. My assets are worth $____. My goal is $____ ($1 million? $10 million?). It makes me feel ____ (happy, free, relaxed, scared).

3. My work is fulfilling because ____. I am making the world a better place by ____.

4. My family is thriving and joyful because ____.

5. My friends say I'm ____ (ex: smart, funny, dedicated).

6. My body is healthy because ____ (ex: I exercise and juice daily).

7. My mind is stimulated because ____ (ex: I am learning, doing what I love, studying, reading).

8. My spirit soars because ____.

Now that you can see and feel your goals, it's time to stand in place with your goals and look back on how you got there. From your ideal situation in each category, look at yourself at the beginning of the journey. Visualize what your life looked like "back then," when you wanted true love, a full bank account, or new career. What was the first step you took that started the momentum toward your goal? It was simple, but it created magic; it defined your amazingness. What was it like to start where you are today? How did you do it?

1. Love: When I look back, I see the first step I took toward the love of my dreams. I started where I was by ____ (ex: seeing that I was worth love, getting my hair done and pampering myself, going on that blind date, asking my husband to touch me more).

2. Money: When I look back, I see the first step I took toward the money of my dreams. I started by ____ (ex: redoing my budget, saving 10 percent of my paycheck).

3. Work: When I look back, I see the first step I took toward the work of my dreams. I started by ____ (ex: thanking my boss for the opportunity to shine, quitting my job for a better one, downloading a business plan template for my business, looking into getting a patent for my idea).

4. Family: When I look back, I see the first step I took toward the family life of my dreams. I started by ____ (ex: having the family sit down for dinner together, not working so late, telling my kids how much I love them).

5. Friends: When I look back, I see the first step I took toward the friendships of my dreams. I started by ____ (ex: calling a friend to tell her how much she meant to me, reaching out to a person I admired and started a friendship, offering to buy lunch for a colleague).

6. Body: When I look back, I see the first step I took toward the body of my dreams. I started by ____ (ex: walking the dog, doing ten reps of arm weights, taking the yoga class, being kind to myself).

7. Mind: When I look back, I see the first step I took toward the inquisitive, knowledgeable mind of my dreams. I started by ____ (ex: watching TED talks, signing up for that class, joining a book club).

8. Spirit: When I look back, I see the first step I took toward the inner life of my dreams. I started by ____ (ex: becoming more aware of my breath, praying, meditating, reading inspirational stories).

The beauty of this exercise is that you get to see yourself where you want to be *and* review where you started. You then get to give yourself the gift of action, insight, and evidence in the world for your genius and your dreams. This is where the water steeps the tea leaves, where the "rubber meets the road," and where you started where you were today, in good faith, wading through life, closing in on your dreams.

> What you get by achieving your goals is not as important as what you become by achieving your goals.
>
> —JOHANN WOLFGANG VON GOETHE

5

Turn a Burden into a Blessing

A Cup of Heaven-Scented Jasmine Blossoms

Leave out my name from the gift if it be a burden,
but keep my song.

—RABINDRANATH TAGORE

Inspiration: Yin Zhen or "Silver Needle." Alone, *Zhen* means "precious, truth, truth in being, authenticity." Yin Zhen is the purest form of white tea; only the tiny new buds are used to make it, no leaves, just sweetly hued potential in the form of a bright, young tea bud.

Yin Zhen comes from ancient tea trees that line the peaked mountains in Fujian, China. Spring harvests yield the best white teas. In March or early April, tea workers in flowery dresses, carrying handmade reed baskets, quietly harvest the unopened white tea buds as the climbing sun illuminates their fine downiness. Evaporating moisture rises like wet smoke from the petite crystalline tea leaves.

At the foot of the mountain is the drying house—an airy structure with a small fire built on the carefully cleaned stone floor. There the downy buds are steamed, which arrests oxidization, sealing the buds' pure essence against time. Afterward, the freshly steamed tea buds are gently, softly, mindfully mixed by hand with white night-blooming jasmine blossoms. As the tea buds dry from their quick steam bath, they absorb the scent of the jasmine and become the perfect carrying companion for the sweet spirit of the flower.

The silver needles of Yin Zhen remind me to purify my thoughts and to reflect on the truth that so many of the burdens that have weighed me down actually have been the means to attaining the strength to uncover my biggest blessings.

Before long, Sage and I outgrew the tea cart. Sage got too big for the hiking backpack I wore as I served my customers their tea lattes. Early in the morning rush, Sage would grow bored and entertain himself by hitting me on the head as I worked. He wanted to play and he made my customers laugh, but the cuteness was not conducive to a calm work attitude. The breaking point came when a new customer was asking me about one of my more delicately scented blends and Sage spit up on top of my head. Trying to be cool as I wiped the curdled milk from my coarse, kinky hair, I realized the tea cart was over. Still, I spent a few weeks chasing him around the store, pulling him out of clothing racks and peeling him off customers, until I realized we were going to have to make some changes in the business model.

In my stint at the tea cart, I'd gotten a lot of love for my blends. Creating the unique flavors was fulfilling and sharing them with others was exhilarating. Now it was time to systematically develop my own line of teas and take my business to the next level. For advice, I contacted some industry experts, since I had passion for the leaf but didn't know how to develop a brand. I was onto a spirit, a vibe that hadn't been tapped yet in the tea business. The English had high tea and tiny sandwiches; the Japanese had Zen tea ceremonies and quiet formality. I could offer fun, flair, and exoticism. To create and stake my claim in the world of tea, and to introduce people to my distinctive product, I wanted to throw Gypsy Tea Parties with tea and belly dancers. Yeah! Sir Thomas Lipton, who created Lipton tea, used to have "Tea Parades" through the streets to celebrate and market his teas, so maybe Gypsy Tea Parties could be the modern equivalent.

I subscribed to the main supplier tea journal, called everyone with an ad in the pages, and spoke with tea brokers from India, China, Africa, and Sri Lanka. I asked loads of dumb questions and marveled at the answers, filling notebooks with leaf grades, kilogram measurements, organic versus conventional growing methods, and workings of the auction system. Each detail inspired me to find out more. I was already in love with tea and now I fell in love with its history and the tea business. I traded stories with the new friends I met over the phone, scrambling over and around language barriers. Traders shared tales of market crashes and global shortages along with anecdotes about the vintages of certain teas, just as if they were fine wines. After a few weeks, I felt like part of a fascinating community. No one bothered to ask how big my company was, how many years I was in business, or if I even *had* a business yet. I told them my idea, and their enthusiasm made me feel like a welcome member of the complex, and at the time exclusive, trade.

One importer insisted I read a certain report, a market research document, if I was serious about the tea business, and he gave me the phone number of Brian, the expert behind it. Brian charged $300 for his tea report, so I was fairly sure I could live without it as I was still scraping money together to buy the actual tea. But I called anyway and a receptionist answered, "Sage Report. How may I direct your call?" "*Sage Report?*" I repeated in disbelief. I believe in synchronicity and could not ignore this one. I decided to stall on a few bills in order to free up the cash for the *Sage Report*.

A few days later, the hand-bound report arrived along with a voucher for "one free hour of consulting." Free was in my budget! I called, and this time Brian himself answered the phone.

He wasn't gentle with his answers to my questions about starting a new line. "There will be thousands of new entries into the tea market in the next decade," he said matter-of-factly.

That was discouraging. I would be fighting for my livelihood with thousands of other companies that probably had resources and degrees and training to back them up. What was I thinking? The idea that I had another mountain to climb settled in my gut. But I had time left on my free hour, so I asked, "Well, then, what would you do if you were me?"

He surprised me, saying, "There's only one you. Name the company after yourself and become the Martha Stewart of tea. Your name is cool. It's very exotic. Trust me on this one. Being authentic in an overcrowded marketplace—being the real you— will pay off."

I shook my head. "My *name*?"

He was firm. "Your name. Take this seriously. There is nothing new under the sun, and your name will make you unique."

I hung up and walked out to the front porch to sit and think. My name had been a thorn in my side my whole life. No one could pronounce it. Every year on the first day of school, the teacher would stop, stare at the roster with a puzzled look, and stutter, "Zaheena Muh . . . Muhzoooka?" All frizzy hair and buckteeth, I would shrink in my seat as all of the kids laughed.

I was named after my great-aunt Zena, Grandma Maria's sister. My mom haphazardly added the *h*, as if it needed to be more original. She hoped I could one day go by a single name like her idol, Cher. On its own, Zena would have called undue attention to my natural weirdness, but that added *h* really threw people.

"Zaheena?"

"No, Zhena."

"Sheeena . . . ? Oh! Like Sheena Easton?"

"Close. Zzzzzhhh." I'd lean on the sound. "Like Dr. Zhivago."

"Geeeenah . . ."

"Perfect," I'd say, letting us both off the hook.

Why would I use this burdensome tongue twister as a brand? This tea consultant was smart enough to have a huge report that people paid hundreds of dollars for, but Gypsy Tea Company was so easy to say and it was memorable. I reached for perspective.

I remembered that in her Ukrainian village, Aunt Zena was Queen of the Gypsies because she had two cows, the sweetest blackberry wine for miles, and a small altar room that villagers would visit to pray to Saint Sarah and the Virgin Mary. Maybe I should step up and embrace the legacy of my namesake.

In Persian, my name means "beauty." In Ukrainian, fittingly, "woman." In Chinese, my name translates to "truth," and Yin Zhen is my favorite of the white teas. Zhen's multiple meanings of "truth," "authentic," and "truth in being" connected deeply to my pursuit of authenticity, which for me was what tea was about. All that the company was meant to embody was actually hidden like an obvious secret in my name.

But in spite of this expert advice, I still thought no one would care what it meant if they couldn't even pronounce it. So I opted to apply for the trademark "Gypsy Tea Company" instead of "Zhena's Gypsy Tea."

When I received a letter back from the United States Patent and Trademark Office, I made a cup of tea and sat down in order to make a ceremony of opening the envelope. It felt very official and *smart* to get a letter from the USPTO from Washington, DC, delivered all the way out in the sticks of Matilija Canyon. I took a sip of tea and savored the anticipation of being officially granted my very own *trademark*.

I nearly dropped my cup when I read, "We are unable to award you a trademark for 'The Gypsy Tea Company' as Gypsy and Tea are both generic terms and do not have any unique designations, therefore you are not able to trademark two generic terms together." Huh? Generic! My heritage is ANYTHING BUT generic! Gypsy tea parties were MY big idea, after all! It came in a VISION, Mr. USPTO! How ridiculous, I thought, that some lawyer in DC could tell me my heritage was TOO GENERIC to trademark. Yes, I was mad. Mad, mad, and mad.

The Roma people, commonly known as Gypsies, originated in India over a thousand years ago. They traveled through Russia and Eastern Europe, and into Western Europe and Spain. The epitome of global citizens, they were a courageous traveling people, the only culture in the world that didn't see any one country as their home, but the whole world as their home.

I had only good associations with the word, but as a teenager had been stricken to learn that Gypsy could be a slanderous term for people of Roma descent. I was eager to retake Gypsy and infuse it with all the good associations of my people. To me, it meant both whimsy and strength. I was proudly descended from, and related to, Moscow circus performers, musicians, animal trainers, and fine wood craftsmen. The women in my family were all like Grandma Maria—healers, herbalists, fortune-tellers, and medicine women. Gypsies are possessors and safekeepers of passion, artisans of music and healing potions, lovers of nature, fiercely independent, celebrators of life, imaginative storytellers, colorful dressers, skilled craftsmen of caravans, creators of flamenco, and readers of palms and tea leaves.

After I gathered myself, I thought back to the tea consultant's advice to use my name to make my company unique. He hadn't grown up with my name, so he didn't see all the baggage it carried that had kept me from putting it in my trademark application. To him, it was just a unique and memorable name.

"Zhena's Gypsy Tea," I said aloud.

I had always wanted to change my name, but maybe I could reclaim it instead, the way I wanted to reclaim the word *Gypsy*. Even if no one could pronounce it, at least they wouldn't forget it.

That guy with the *Sage Report* is my hero for helping me turn my name from a burden into an authentic company identity. People would be drawn to it because there is a real woman behind the tea, standing by her name and legacy, claiming it after all.

Turn a Burden into a Blessing

*Mantra of the Cup: Today there are no burdens,
only blessings.*

What burden are you carrying that is a blessing in disguise? I had wanted so badly to change my name, but when the time came to stake my claim in the world, my name came through and really helped me out. (Thanks, Mom!) What if each burden in your life is actually a thinly cloaked blessing just waiting for you to uncover its true meaning? What if each challenge or burden is actually moving you closer to your highest calling?

I have a friend and coaching client, Lori, whose life wasn't going as planned. Her kids had gone off to college and she'd fallen into a deep, sad empty-nest depression. Then she lost her teaching job in the California budget cuts, and the family had to rely on only her husband's income for their three kids' college tuition. Without a job, she had a lot of time on her hands and she spent a lot of that time worrying a lot about money.

On her fiftieth birthday, she looked around her empty house and realized that one of the things she missed the most were the long summer days with her kids at their family lemonade stand. She took all of her sadness, loneliness, and fear over a lack of money and poured it into making a batch of lemonade. And then she had the idea of starting a lemonade company from the recipe she and her kids used. Barely believing she was doing it, she started bottling her lemonade and delivering samples to stores and restaurants all over Ojai. She put her story on her label.

People (especially moms) really could relate to her story, everyone loved the lemonade, and orders started flying in. Her empty nest was soon filled with deliveries, laughter, sips of sweet lemonade, and excited employees. Her kids even came back in the summers and worked for her. She now has a thriving business—Lori's Original Lemonade.

After losing her job, Lori could have descended into self-pity, but by shifting her point of view, she opted to make something positive out of her situation. She is not only helping to pay for her kids' college, she will probably employ them when they graduate. Now that's a creative way to get the kids back! Her burden was an empty nest, no job, and worries about the future, but she turned her losses into a blessing and stepping-stone to creating her own job and jobs for others. Lori often asks me if what she's doing is real, and I tell her it's real because she made it so. She works her tail off, but she's one of the happiest people I know.

Exercise: Repurposing Burdens

In the spirit of discovering how a burden in your life is a blessing in disguise, this exercise will allow you to shift your circumstance into opportunity—and even make miracles. Think of something that has been "weighing" you down, "holding" you back, or keeping you from being happy. It could be your weight, a bill, anything that feels heavy to you. Close your eyes and imagine this burden. See it, examine its every detail. The more detail you notice, the better. If it's a bill, follow it to the issuer; if it's a grievance with someone at work, see its effects fully; if it's a few pounds of extra hip matter, imagine that weight as a thing.

Now become very aware of the burden, its attributes, appearance, and any other details. Really look at it as if you're in biology class, seeing it under a microscope for the first time. Ask yourself these questions.

1. What is the burden and is it real? Name it. (Example: My colleague at work)

2. How is the burden affecting my life? (She takes too long to approve my projects and it is making me lose business)

3. What result is that giving me? (Less commission)

4. What result would I like to have? (More commission)

5. If this burden is a gatekeeper to my growth, what lesson is it asking me to learn? (I need to communicate better to her about why I need her to speed up her process)

6. How can I approach and see the burden for the life lesson it is rather than the heavy burden it feels like? (I could offer her help to get the approval process done faster)

7. What is the burden teaching me? (That the frustration I feel is because I haven't offered my communication or help to my colleague)

8. What is the blessing in this? (I can make more commission by learning clearer communication skills and by offering a helping hand)

Answering these questions enables you to shift your perception of a burden so you see facets of it that are a blessing. You release your mind and spirit from being weighed down so you can examine the lesson in that burden. It may take some time to grasp the lesson, but as soon as you examine the hidden blessing it is showing you, the awareness takes hold of you and you are that much closer to your dream.

Is there something you've always wanted to change in your life that you can reexamine and "repurpose" into a blessing? I'd LOVE to hear about it! Email me at Zhena@Zhena.tv and tell me all about it. ☺

The burden of self is lightened when I laugh at myself.

—RABINDRANATH TAGORE

6

Pluck the Positive

A Cup of "Good Morning, Sunshine!"

*There is a great deal of poetry and fine sentiment
in a chest of tea.*

—RALPH WALDO EMERSON

Inspiration: A basic black tea with no flavors added, no oils, nothing extra. Today, my Bed and Breakfast black tea, is a blend of grade A, fair-trade black tea leaves from the Uva province of Sri Lanka, the Nilgiri Mountains of southern India, and the Yunnan province of China. But it started out as simply a Sri Lankan tea, because I could afford only one chest of it. From that one chest, I had to develop an entire product line.

Sipping this morning blend today, I can't help but reminisce about the importance it had for me when I was first starting out—it meant the world. This tea was the pure, clean canvas on which I could paint infinite colors and possibilities. These leaves carry flavor notes of raisin, tobacco flower, rum, hay, and the balmy afternoon rains of Sri Lanka. The tea also has a bit of caramel on the palate, with high notes of optimism and promise. The caffeine content is fairly high, waking you up, kicking you in the butt, and sharpening your senses to how amazing you are and what more you can be.

If you sip this tea in a quiet moment, you can taste hints of hope. You may hear children laughing as they play cricket barefoot in the monsoon-drenched roads of hill country. Traditionally drunk with thick fresh milk and sticky raw sugar, this tea is the epitome of potentiality, rich in character yet waiting still for you to put your own spin on it—making it your own—perhaps your local honey, a dash of brown sugar, or even sweet cream. Maybe even a gratitude prayer . . . its sweetness opens the heart to possibility.

This tea was born out of intention and dedication. It was my first sign that I would start a tea company and possibly even *succeed*.

My very first crate of tea arrived in a UPS truck that creaked and teetered up the rocky driveway to my cabin. For months, I had scraped together the little bits of profits from my tea cart, until I could place my order with a kindly Sri Lankan tea broker. It was finally here. I ran out to greet the deliveryman. The afternoon sun flared off the metal strapping on the nondescript wooden crate as he wheeled it to my door and into my living room, smiling like Santa, as I squealed and oohed over it.

The label said, "Organic Black Tea," and the name of the estate where it had been grown, Idulgashinna. There was also a small painting of a ladybug sitting on a green tea leaf on the side. "Ladybugs are good luck," my grandma had said. An image of her with her big hoop earrings, colorful dress, and scarf over her hair came back to me. We were standing in her garden as she caught a ladybug for me, put it on my finger, and said, "Zenitska, now blow on it and make a wish. When it flies away, your wish will come true."

This tea chest was full of potential—it provided me a base for developing new blends, a chance for me to sell more than a few ounces of tea at a time. This crate of leaves could transform me from a tea cart owner to a tea *company* owner. It was a treasure chest promising a better future for my son and me. As I lifted the lid, I felt I was opening something precious, monumental. I said a prayer as I did so.

Inside the thin, balsa wood walls of the crate was a sea of perfect reddish-black tea leaves, all uniform in size and shape. Their color was rich and their scent transporting. The crate itself gave off a scent of soil freshly soaked by sweet island rain, filling my small living room and infusing me with awe. I could *feel* the energy of the people who had carefully harvested these leaves. I had to learn who they were and make sure they knew how grateful I was.

The purchase of the crate felt to me like a spiritual contract between tea laborer and tea maker. After my initial high of seeing so many tea leaves at once, I ran to the phone and called the importer from whom I had bought the shipment. I asked him every question this side of the Pacific about the people behind this tea. Who are they? Where do they come from? How much money do we pay them? Are you sure they get the money? Is fair trade for real? Is there a way to talk to them? Do they have email? Where are their kids when they are plucking tea? What are their houses like? Do they know who is buying their tea? Do they know that what they are doing is just so . . . SPECIAL?!

"Zhena, I can tell you are sincere and want to know. My advice is that you sell more, then buy more, and then pay for a trip to go see the workers directly, yourself. It will answer *all* your questions. I can give you industry statistics, but if you want to really dedicate yourself to tea, the real benefit comes from knowing the workers and their craft *personally*."

My mind leaped across the Pacific. That was it! I would go! My mom could watch Sage, and I could actually meet the people who made this intoxicating tea. I would tell them how much I loved their work and appreciated it. I would invite them to California to visit, to Christmas dinner. Sage and their kids could grow up together. As I visualized my very own global family growing, a circle unbroken, my Gypsy soul caught fire. Wanderlust and curiosity emboldened me to want to share my life with the women who made such beauty in the world.

After the initial rush faded and I stopped jumping around like a caffeinated Chihuahua, I sat down and calculated how many crates I would have to buy, blend into one-pound bags, and then sell to cover the trip. I slumped in my little office chair at the numbers. After living costs, cost of goods and bills, it would take a hundred or more of these crates to pay for a trip to the tea fields in Sri Lanka.

All of the sparkling possibilities of meeting the tea workers faded back into my spreadsheet, into the black-and-white desolation of the bottom line. I hadn't even sold one pound from my first crate yet. Seventy-seven pounds to go on crate number one. Seventy-seven hundred pounds to go to reach crate one hundred.

The fire in my belly was momentarily damped down by the seemingly colossal number.

Nonetheless, I continued to research and bug every tea importer who would answer the phone to learn everything I could about the women tea workers. I sensed they were like me, wanting to make a good life for their kids. I sipped the black tea and closed my eyes, imagining their hands touching each leaf carefully and mindfully. I felt like I was in my very own version of *Like Water for Chocolate*, in which the energy of the cook is transmitted into the food she makes, and those who eat her meals are transformed by her emotions. This tea made me *happy*.

Just as the energy of the tea workers had touched these leaves, my own energy would touch them, too, as I carefully, mindfully blended them into my potions. I wanted to honor the hard work of the women in the tea fields and infuse positive energy into the blends that my customers would then imbibe. With my son as a daily reminder of the grace I enjoyed, I held the women of the tea fields in my mind's eye. Their work was saving my life and they motivated me to work harder, sell more, build faster.

One tea crate represents 193,600 individual plucks of a woman's hand. She carefully plucks only the top two leaves and the bud in a precise movement called a "fine plucking," which cannot be accomplished by machine. Her daily quota is 8 kilograms or 17.6 pounds of tea a day, which is about 16,000 individual "fine plucks."

The tea plucker perches on steep hillsides, at altitudes of five thousand feet and higher, a tarp tied over her sari to keep it dry in the heavy mists, a large basket on her back held in place by a strap on her forehead. As she fills the basket, its weight increases. Her petite body moves up and down the faint, narrow trails carved by her sandaled feet during the last harvest, six weeks before. As the tea workers pluck, they chat, their singsong voices lilting, their laughter rising and falling.

They focus on the newly emerging celadon-green tea buds and the dewy, still soft leaves just beneath. The bud holds the greatest flavor potential in its tightly wrapped folds; the new leaves are the most malleable and easiest to roll. Lithe hands whisk away only these, the newest, freshest, and most inspired parts of the plant, masterfully avoiding the older, bitter leaves below.

There is a Gypsy saying that goes, "The easiest thing to start is the hardest to finish." One night, particularly discouraged after pounding the pavement and returning home to my tally and the mostly full crate, I wished the crate away. My calling suddenly felt like a ridiculous fairy tale. That morning, Sage had a fever and we'd spent most of the day in the hospital getting tests. Reminded of his frailty, I felt guilty for wanting this business and for thinking of traveling without him to the tea fields. After we left the hospital, I tried to split my focus from Sage in order to sell some tea, knowing that the medical bill for the day would be enormous. I'd spent hours attempting to persuade my list of cafés to place orders, but none had. I'd struggled to sell a single pound and saw the long haul ahead of me to empty the crate as interminable. I could quit now and the crate could be an end table, I thought, a reminder that I wasn't good at finishing things.

The next morning was freezing. I woke up curled around

Sage with the comforter over our heads. I could see my breath. I tucked Sage deeply into the bed and boiled water on the stove. As the water began to bubble in the little saucepan (I didn't have a teakettle yet), I looked for some of the loose tea and realized my jar was empty. Walking over to the crate, I used a butter knife to pull the lid up, and the scent of the tea rose up and enveloped me once again. It *hugged* me. My nose tickled, and I felt substantially less alone. I marveled at the sensation of joy deep in my belly and smiled. I scooped a teaspoonful of the leaves, added them to a clear cup of hot water, and they opened and released their flavor in wisps. My tea importer had said, "It's extra work, but a fine plucking makes the most beautiful character in the cup. While a rough plucking is easier, it makes bitter, tannic tea with an unforgiving character."

Sipping the shimmering golden-brown liquor filled me with optimism. The women in the tea fields held a lesson for me in the tips of their skilled fingers and in the spirit with which they harvested the leaves. They had dedicated sixteen thousand perfectly synchronized motions a day to deliver this precious tonic, focusing solely on the top two leaves and bud, leaving the coarse ones behind. I had to let go of my own rough leaves—my doubts and fears—in order to make my life positive.

With a renewed sense of clarity, I sipped the tea, watching the sun peek over the canyon mountain walls. As it rose over the chaparral-lined ridge, I said, "Good morning, sunshine." Gone were the shadowy, bitter doubts from the night before.

If tea pickers could make the effort to pluck the finest parts of the plant every single day for so many decades, I could match their optimism and earnestness in my commitment to selling seventy-seven hundred pounds. Their fine plucking and energetic imprint lifted me up from across the world. Their tea helped me generate an unprecedented level of motivation and gratitude. I closed my eyes and visualized my cabin with one hundred empty crates piled to the ceiling.

Pluck the Positive

Mantra of the Cup: I am an alchemist, transforming each mood into gold and each thought into sunlight.

The most successful people have a knack for "plucking the positive." They seek out the sunshine, the choicest leaves of a plant. They look for solutions, daring to believe life is a friendly endeavor and that failure offers the chance to grow. They harvest the finest aspects of life, leaving the rough ones behind for compost. They see the silver lining and repeatedly trace it with their focus.

As you awaken each morning, you can decide, "Will this be a fine day or a rough day?" When you use your skills and act from the heart, when you show the world your willingness and optimism, you get to write your day rather than be written by it. Do you tend to pluck the most positive aspects of your day to dwell on, or do you tend to allow your day to go unchecked while unintentionally allowing the "rough" parts of it get to you? Waking up happy is not always a given. Heartbreak makes us hurt, and the loss of love or loved ones weighs heavily. All the pain that comes with being human can crush our optimism if we don't work actively to create our own hope.

You have to be intentional to spark the day's inspiration. Mindfully carve out a few moments to breathe, to look for something to appreciate, even during a harried morning. All the small actions you take deserve appreciation: how you wake up, breathe, pack lunches, get the kids to school, dress yourself, take your vitamins, open the door for others. Appreciation is an activity. Cultivate your ability to consistently "pluck the positive."

Back when I received that first crate of tea, I was teetering on the edge, struggling to turn a few tea leaves into a thriving life for my ailing son and me. I was living well below the poverty line. Every morning I awoke and worked hard to fill my field of vision with vivid prospects of potential happiness and success instead of the harsh alternatives. I could not allow loss and failure to infuse me with fear, stopping my dreams cold, so I composted the darker, bitter parts of me into fuel for my tender, green hopes and dreams that were emerging and reaching toward the light. This practice was a survival strategy for Sage's sake, but in the process, it led me out of darkness and into light.

Waking up to your potential is like waking up each morning. Buddha said, "Every morning we are born again, what we do today is what matters most." Each brand-new day holds new options for joy. You only have memories of yesterdays and hopes of tomorrows—but today, you have yourself and every single sovereign thought that can flow through your heart, into your mind, and out into the world. Practicing appreciation, seeking positive thoughts, and dwelling on what is right in your life are all actions that swiftly move you toward your dreams.

Each morning I drink this black tea and say a gratitude prayer. It only takes thirty seconds. If I allow myself to get too busy and not offer this prayer, the day isn't as good. The precious thoughts of gratitude and appreciation have to be rustled up and remembered. The sacred doesn't come right out and hit us over the head when we forget about it. Even though I wake up and immediately think about the day's schedule and responsibilities, the moment I take with my grandma's cup and a nice long steep of tea wakes me up to possibilities. This simple practice shifts my mood from automatic to mindful and sets me up to look at the bright side all day.

Exercise: Plucking the Positive

Anne Lamott writes, "Take the action, the insight will follow." That is definitely the lesson of this cup. By generating appreciation even when you don't feel grateful, you allow your heart and mind to seek out the positive aspects of your life. When you focus on the positive energy of anything, it will multiply.

One of my mentors says, "That which you pay attention to grows." If you are paying attention to what you lack, it will grow. The trick to changing your life is to choose to envision what you want in your life as being already here in it. Visualizing the reality of your dreams will allow you to transmute darkness into light. The lesson of the tea workers is simple: Show up every day and perform a fine plucking. Focus only on those fresh, new top two leaves and bud so you can see them clearly above the coarse leaves below. By shifting what you look for, you will create a day that has the qualities of mindfulness and appreciation.

A daily gratitude prayer, recited while you sip your morning cup of tea, affirms your commitment to the positive in your life. Say thank you for three things each morning as you sip your tea. This practice focuses your keen eye on your very own fresh top two leaves and a bud. When gratitude emanates from you into the world, others feel your positivity and reflect their thanks right back to you, creating a feedback loop of grace.

One of my prayers is, "Thank you, God, for this day and for this miraculous cup of tea. Thank you for my family and my health and for the opportunity to be of service." If my mind is still unquiet, still reaching for things to worry about—unbalanced budgets, unanswered questions, unresolved regrets, and the unrelenting march of time—I breathe in the fragrant steam again and dig deeper. "Thank you for running water, thank you for the sun and the hibiscus blooming in my yard." Anything I can think of, I say "thank you" for it. Soon enough the bitterness of any negativity exits stage left and I'm in a new play.

Turn your face to the sun and the shadows fall behind you.

—MAORI PROVERB

7

Get to the "Heart" of the Matter

A Cup of Organic Roses

In doing something, do it with love,
or never do it at all.

—MAHATMA GANDHI

Inspiration: The healing power of roses. Roses are the queen of flowers. My grandmother's vast city-lot garden was lined with roses, and she made jelly from the pink petals. She also simmered the buds in sugar water and allowed me to take tiny sips when I was a child. Nostalgia inspired me to bring the romantic, heart-healing essence of rose oil and rose petals into an organic blend of black tea with flavor notes of burgundy wine, black plum, a hint of wildfire smoke, and wisps of fresh rosebuds drying in sea air.

Rose tea is full-bodied, takes milk and honey well, and keeps its floral complexity through many steepings. I make a Gypsy Love rose tea that is recalibrating to brew and drink. When thoughts and worries threaten to drown out the voice of the heart, rose tea reminds us that acting from the heart requires an understanding of the heart's sensual language, which might not always make sense to the mind.

To make rose tea, fresh, newly plucked tea leaves are slowly dried with rose petals over twenty-four hours. Rose tea is a simple blend to make once you have the perfect roses to sweeten the light, astringent, high-grown leaves. We mix black teas from southern India and Sri Lanka with a touch of golden tea buds from Yunnan—a still-sacred region where the air is clean and tea growers quietly produce the slightly smoky flavor by gently tossing the leaves in handmade reed baskets over glowing pine wood embers.

When I first started making my own tea blends, I used roses from my yard, supplementing them with deliciously aromatic rosebuds from Greece. For such a simple blend, with only four ingredients, the quality of the roses is of the utmost importance. They have to be sweet, intensely aromatic, and organic. Organic teas were a new idea at the time, but from the start, using organic ingredients was a core aspect of my vision. It was especially important to me to find organic roses because roses are sprayed more than any other type of flower for commercial production.

After committing to the next stage of growing my business, I sold the tea cart to my best friend from high school and banked my bets on making tea blends and selling them to other cafés and restaurants. I sublet a small section of a two-hundred-square-foot warehouse in Ojai from an angel of a woman who made exquisite freeze-dried flower arrangements for upscale department stores like Nordstrom and Neiman Marcus. Between my tea and her flowers, we created a rapturous fragrance of petals, herbs, and spices while Sage happily crawled around on the pieces of remnant carpet at my feet. Blending and packing small samples of tea, I got to work building a wholesale business.

I took Sage with me to deliver samples to every local café, restaurant, spa, and hotel in the Ojai Valley and Santa Barbara. At the time, most of the chefs and managers didn't yet know how to serve and steep artisan loose-leaf teas, so it was fun to pioneer these visually beautiful and palate-pleasing products. The simple black and green teas tasted delicious, but the most visually stunning and sense-intoxicating was the rose petal black tea. It became the favorite of chefs and spa owners.

For Gypsy Love rose tea, I blended three black teas together, added a few drops of organic essential rose oil, tossed in sundried roses from my yard, and gently hand-mixed it all in a large stainless steel bowl—the kind my grandmother had used when she mixed sweet dough for her famous braided bread, which she baked for her congregation. As I blended the freshly dried petals into the tea, I listened to Gypsy music, which together with the scent of roses floating in the air made me even more of a hopeless romantic.

As a single mom, I craved romance. This tea fed the amorous dreamer in me, so I blended a lot of it as I prepared to throw my first Gypsy Tea Party. A defining vision for my business from the beginning, the parties were the next step in my plan to expand. I put up flyers around town advertising the party, which I would hold on my friend Meg's back porch at her art gallery. A belly dance troupe leader I'd studied with agreed to dance, and a few palm readers, tarot readers, and tea leaf readers would join us.

As soon as the flyers went up, I got calls from jewelry designers, musicians, dance troupes, painters, sculptors, movement artists, and even a flame thrower who swallowed a sword—all of them wanted to join the caravan of my Gypsy Tea Party. More than two hundred people showed up, sipped and bought my tea blends, danced, got their palms read, bought art and jewelry, and asked when the next party would be. It was nothing short of a miracle. My blends were a hit and, by the time it was over, I had a slew of orders. Gypsy Love was the best seller by far.

I had found an investor, which was exactly what I needed to make the leap from the cart to a bigger business. He brought in a couple other local investors and helped me to incorporate the business into a legal entity. My small wholesale accounts were growing and, with orders coming in from the community tea drinkers who had attended the tea party, I geared up for high production. My little rosebushes couldn't fill this many orders, so I scoured the Internet for bulk prices on organic roses and rose oil—and ran right into a hard wall of reality. Preparing my signature blend and best seller, Gypsy Love, was going to break the bank. I couldn't make a profit on this tea without raising the price substantially. Did my customers love it enough to pay a high premium?

I asked my main investor what I should do about the expensive rose petals—and hit a second wall. He suggested—well, demanded, really—that I lower costs by going nonorganic.

My heart sank.

"Look, I've done my research," he said. "Organic rosebuds are six times the cost of nonorganic. Your rose oil is up to seventy times the cost of the artificial stuff. All tea is inherently organic. I mean, if it grows, it's organic, right?"

He was a successful businessman because he put the bottom line first. He was essentially right. He urged me to stop clinging to my ideal. I needed to be smart. Even though it hurt my heart and my head, I ordered a crate of conventionally grown tea, some conventional roses, and artificial rose oil.

When the tea arrived and the UPS man had kindly unloaded the crate in the middle of the warehouse floor, I just looked at the crate and circled it a few times. It didn't give me the same sensation I got from a crate of organic tea, which always put a smile on my face and lit a small flame of excitement in my chest. Imagining the women plucking the perfect leaves in a happy and healthy organic environment made me feel connected to them, sharing in the effort of bringing pure tea to market. By contrast, anybody could buy and sell this conventional tea—it was a commodity. I didn't know who had grown it or from which garden it came. There was no specific name on the crate. It simply said, in black and white: "China OP2801." There was no ladybug painted on the wood like the organic crates from Idulgashinna Estate had. It felt impersonal, common, unremarkable. But it was less than a quarter of the cost of organic, meaning I could "buy low and sell high"—every businessperson's dream, right?

When the artificial rose flavor and the nonorganic roses arrived, I was surprised to find I could barely detect a flavor difference. Yet I still felt that it was wrong for me to use them. It was just a feeling, I told myself, but that feeling grew into a heartsickness that wouldn't let me rest. I needed to make money, but the feeling about what was right and wrong for my teas and for me grew stronger, even though I didn't voice it. Torn between doing what I felt was right and what my investor said was smart business, I wondered how I could separate my personal beliefs from my business. I never bought conventional food, so why would I sell conventional tea? Back then, anyone could write "organic" on a label without USDA approval, so maybe in fact organic wasn't real after all? Doubt swirled inside me; confusion followed. Second-guessing yourself is a sure sign you're off track, but I didn't know that yet.

My commitment to organic ingredients was not quite fully formed at this point, but my intuition was pushing me in that direction. Still, I examined the numbers on the nonorganic blend over and over. The tea looked all right. The money was astronomically better. But I felt my love for my beautiful rose tea blend fade. After all, it was called "Gypsy Love," not "Gypsy Bank Balance." How could I justify spending so much more without a way to explain why, other than it felt right and was better for the environment way over in Sri Lanka, Greece, and Bulgaria? It mattered to me, but if it didn't matter to my investors then the discord could leave me businessless. I had to get moving.

I blended a batch of organic and nonorganic rose tea and took it to the Specialty Tea Institute. The director of curriculum there had heard about my use of essential oils in teas, and he asked me to teach my methods to their members. I decided to test my theory that organic-natural would taste different from conventional-artificial to their well-educated palates. So I conducted a blind tasting and tasked my students to tell me which tea was organic. To my surprise, the questionnaires came back 50 percent correct and 50 percent wrong, with the comments slightly skewed toward the artificial for tasting "brighter."

Later, in the institute's bathroom, I took a good look at myself in the mirror. The evidence was clear: I could lower the cost and nobody would taste the difference. If I put so much weight on my feelings, maybe I wasn't cracked up for business after all. I had hung my hat on those organic roses and now the data proved me wrong.

A tall, elegantly dressed woman from the class walked in and, seeing me, paused. She was a food scientist and one of the most engaged students.

"You were thrown by the results of the test," she ventured.

I had to laugh at myself, saying, "I was expecting validation, and instead I got debunked."

"You know, I make both natural-organic and artificial flavors for a living at a flavor house," she said. "There is a difference. It's subtle, but it's decisive. If you want my opinion, that is."

My heart perked up. "You have no idea!"

"It's the sun," she said. "While the artificial flavor might be 'nature identical,' it was never grown in nature. It was made in a beaker, fed by fluorescent light, not sunlight. Many people might not detect the difference, but those of us who know, know. And as you grow your business, more and more people will know what sun tastes like—but most important, you will know you are doing what is best. I think that can be sensed in tea leaves, roses, just about anything that people put in their bodies."

I thanked her and hurried back to the warehouse. Later that week I told the investor that I couldn't sell nonorganic teas even if it meant greater profits. He met with the other investors, and they decided they all wanted to sell their shares. Just like that. I didn't know what I was going to do. Instead of helping me sell tea, the shareholders were giving me a vote of no confidence; I felt rejected, deserted, and foolish. Without money coming in from them, company revenues weren't yet enough to sustain my warehouse and trade show expenses, much less the small paycheck that I relied on as the only employee. I'd have to close.

I called my former neighbor, Ava, who had become a good friend and confidante since the day she'd brought me the pot of lentil soup. She had moved part-time to Hawaii and was living among Kona coffee farms, but we were still in touch.

"He told me it just wasn't good business," I moaned.

"And he's a good businessman," she said. "But, honey, you're trying to make a new kind of business. I see the negative effects of pesticides out here on the plantations in Hawaii, but most people don't spend time on farms. For them, it's hard to see how chemicals hurt more than bugs."

"Ava, I don't know what to do."

"Why don't you ask me for help?"

"Help!" I squeaked.

Within a month, Ava flew in from Hawaii, called a meeting of my investors, and offered to buy their shares. Her commitment ensured that our business would be unconventional forever. In this moment, the money and the mission of our tea company aligned and brought heart into the forefront of how we did things.

I kept the crate of conventional tea, the pouches of nonorganic roses, and the small jar of artificial rose oil in the middle of the warehouse as a reminder that whenever I have a tough decision to make, my heart knows what's right and wise, what's rooted in my values, and what's fed by my faith.

Get to the Heart of the Matter

Mantra of the Cup: I listen to the language of my heart.
It shows me the way.

Your head says, "You can't taste the sun!" but your heart knows what it knows. Those who love what they do and the products they make illuminate this in every walk of life as well as in all the things they "do for free" because of love. Many years after this Gypsy Love rose tea experience, I met the economist Hazel Henderson at a Global Mind Change Forum. She spoke of the "Love Economy," which measures all we do every day for love—not money. Love is not measured or monetized in any GDP calculation. It's a value exchanged from the heart every day for no pay. You may garden, help a friend move or get through a divorce, care for animals, carry groceries for a neighbor, teach a nephew to tell time, mother and nurture your children and friends, give warm compliments, and serve others tea or food. All that you do for free, from your heart, is the Love Economy. This economy perplexes the "money people."

I believe there is an ultimately powerful return on investment on love. The problem with many money-minded people is that they don't see or believe in love's ROI because they can't easily see it in a spreadsheet or immediately measure it in a balance sheet. When businesspeople look solely for the "bottom line," they make poor decisions. Short-term decisions. Wall Street–style quarterly-report-type decisions. There is no room in their model for the highest return of all—love. Love makes a product transcend the actual material that makes it. Love elevates consuming a product into an experience. The imprint that a founder or product maker has on a product cannot be measured other than through a "feeling" people have with and for the product or service. I used to tell my grocery store buyers, only half jokingly, "I sell love and hope—oh, and the tea comes with it—free of charge!"

All the things we do for love matter. Just because we can't measure the love in a profit-and-loss statement doesn't mean it doesn't exist or carry value. The feeling a product can give us is spirit, love, and consciousness in action—its ultimate value. So many heart-centered businesses end up lifeless—investors invest because they fall in love with something, then their "better judgment" takes hold; they may replace founders with managers who see the spreadsheet and start hacking and slashing to get profits. They ignore the love and eventually lose it. Paper replaces passion. Data replace magic. The obsession with profits drowns out possibilities. When a business loses its love, it loses vitality because numbers, data, and trends can't give love. Only people can. What they don't realize is that data can tell us what happened in the past, but the tug of the heart is actually telling us the future.

Feeling is believing, because seeing can't be fully trusted. We see what we look for, not for what we necessarily feel. Getting to the heart of the matter is required for achieving the ultimate goal—that return on investment on love.

My friend Lisa loves, loves, loves dogs. A massage therapist specializing in animals, she comes to my home, and my dog, Willow, just goes crazy for her; every dog on the planet does. She's like the patron saint of canines and, when she goes to heaven, I'm convinced that God will put her in charge of dog well-being and comfort as her eternal post. A few years back, Lisa was worried over her dachshund, June, who was always in pain due to a back injury. She couldn't bear seeing June suffer, so she found a seamstress and invented a back brace with pressure points. Soon, June was running around playing again like a puppy. Lisa now sells her patented back braces internationally, and dog owners swear by her product.

When I was coaching Lisa on her business, she said, "I don't want to sit at a computer all day because it takes away the time I have to put love into each wiggle-less brace." I asked her how she does this, and she said, a little shyly, "Well, I literally put love into each one before it ships. When someone orders one, I pray into it and massage lavender essential oil into the fabric. I visualize the dog receiving it being healthy and happy. I usually get a picture with the order of the dog, so I envision it running and playing, pain-free." She added, "I also play healing music in the stockroom so each brace is infused with soothing melodies. God, I sound crazy! I've never told anyone that I do this. Do you think it's a good use of my time? I mean, is it good for business when there's so much else to be done?"

"Yes," I said, "undoubtedly, it's the best use of your time. It's the best thing for your business."

Exercise: Loving-Kindness Meditation

Shortly after Sage was born, I discovered meditation as a way to keep myself calm, positive, and focused. My meditation teacher teaches a loving-kindness meditation as the dessert after a tough and salty main course of insight meditation. The soothing delight of this simple, sweet practice is like honey for your tea. Loving-kindness meditation helps you delve into the vast resources of your heart's ability to heal, hone, and honor peace and happiness. Buddha originated the practice in order to increase compassion. I give you a teacup serving of this profound practice here, since I'm a "Buddhist-lite." If it resonates with you, I urge you to go deeper into it, because it works. As long as I cultivate loving-kindness in my heart, my mind will go along with any heart or emotional decisions I make, even if they seem illogical. The less conflict we have between the head and heart, the easier life becomes.

Here are the simple steps for a cupful of loving-kindness to sip from.

1. Find a relaxing, quiet space where you can sit for fifteen minutes. Sit comfortably and breathe deeply until you reach a relaxed state. (When you get comfortable, you can do this anywhere—in a subway, in a board meeting, in line at the bank.)

2. Create or choose a mantra for yourself that reflects the loving-kindness you would like to feel for yourself and others. I use this: "May I be peaceful. May I be free from harm. May I be free of mental and physical suffering. May I be happy and healthy. May I be joyful toward myself and others."

3. Breathe deeply, focusing on your heart. Repeat the mantra in your mind while breathing the energy of the mantra into your heart. Repeat the mantra five times or more.

4. You may feel warmth permeating your chest area and feel well nourished by it. When you do, you are ready to envision someone you love very much. This person will be someone who has never forsaken you, a spiritual leader,

your pastor, Jesus, a saint, or a mentor. Say the mantra to this person: "May you be peaceful. May you be free from harm. May you be free of mental and physical suffering. May you be happy and healthy. May you be joyful toward yourself and others."

5. After you have spent time focusing on this being or person, focus on a person you love in your family—a child, a mate, a sister. Say the mantra to that person, as you envision his or her face. "May you be peaceful. May you be free from harm. May you be free of mental and physical suffering. May you be happy and healthy. May you be joyful toward yourself and others."

6. Now, focus on someone who is a neutral person in your life. Maybe someone at the office or someone who waits on you at your favorite restaurant. Say the mantra to that person in your mind's eye. "May you be peaceful. May you be free from harm. May you be free of mental and physical suffering. May you be happy and healthy. May you be joyful toward yourself and others."

7. Now focus on someone with whom you are angry or have conflict, or someone you need to forgive. Forgiveness doesn't excuse wrongdoing, but it gives you back your own energy that you are expending on the past. If your heart clenches or anger arises, keep going. Say the mantra toward the person and your heart will move toward forgiveness. Repeat the mantra while visualizing this person. "May you be peaceful. May you be free from harm. May you be free of mental and physical suffering. May you be happy and healthy. May you be joyful toward yourself and others."

8. Take the feeling of loving-kindness and envision your-self, the person you love, the neutral person, and the challenging person all receiving your loving-kindness and smiling back at you. Give the mantra to all of them and feel your heart opening toward them.

9. Now take the loving-kindness and the mantra and say it to the world, say it once in each direction around you, toward the four directions—east, west, north, and south.

May this practice bring love into each and every cell of your being. May it open new opportunities for forgiveness for you. When I remember to practice it regularly, my grievances and negative expectations melt away and I find myself having trans-formative exchanges with others and discovering sparkling op-portunities. It also allows me to tap into a deep knowing beyond intellect. May you experience the same.

> I will greet this day with love in my heart. For this is the greatest secret of success in all ventures. Muscle can split a shield and even destroy life itself but only the unseen power of love can open the hearts of man. And until I master this act I will remain no more than a peddler in the marketplace. I will make love my greatest weapon and none on who I call can defend upon its force . . . my love will melt all hearts liken to the sun whose rays soften the coldest clay.
>
> —OG MANDINO

8

Blend What You've Got

A Cup of Liberating Limitations

Your limitations create your sound.

—NORAH JONES

Inspiration: Hot island ginger essential oils that warm the tongue and throat atop the sensation of rich, complex black tea hinting at sharp then sweet notes as they dance across the palate. Ginger invigorates the imagination, strengthens circulation throughout the body, warms the digestive tract, and eases morning sickness in pregnant women. Peach is nostalgic of long-ripened summer days when we had so much more time . . .

My Peach Ginger black tea is a sultry blend of pristine, high-mountain-grown Ceylon black tea from the Idulgashinna Estate in the Uva district, known for its fresh air and mist-strewn peaks etched by tea bushes, massive pine trees, and the faint line of a train track. Organically grown, fresh golden peaches are slowly simmered into a thick, pure extract that fills the mouth with its bold ripeness.

After I had committed to making only organic tea and enjoyed the sensational reception of that Gypsy Tea Party, it was time to expand my line beyond Gypsy Rose and the straight, unblended varieties like Bed and Breakfast. No other tea company in the market had the kind of fun, organic, novelty blends I was creating.

The world was full of inspiration. I wanted to make a tea that tasted like my mom's sweet, salty summer peach cobbler, hot with melting fresh vanilla bean ice cream. A Balinese body masque made of jasmine and cocoa sent my imagination spinning. A heady glass of wine got me wondering if I could use dried Pinot Noir or Sangiovese grapes to build a tea blend that would mimic a fine vintage.

I wanted my teas to do it all: encompass the enchanting art of perfumery and aromatherapy, increase vitality with subtly incorporated healing herbs, and enrapture the senses with indulgent, intriguing flavors. I brought out my aromatherapy and herbal medicine textbooks and used their insights to sketch out new blend ideas inspired by desserts and spa treatments. I categorized these recipe sketches in an orange silk journal that I called my "Book of Dreams."

But as I took the ideas into the blending room, I once again bumped into obstacles that adhering to organic standards imposed. Organic flavorings didn't pack the kind of punch needed to make a tea out of a dessert favorite like Peach Cobbler with Homemade Vanilla Ice Cream Tea; they didn't give enough of a fatty, sensual, sugary mouth feel. My cocoa and jasmine blend was much too subtle, as well, after I'd imagined swirling rich hot cocoa with a sensual jasmine lift on the nose—a sexy potion of sorts. The blend smelled of both but tasted mostly like black tea; the flavors of the scents were lost in translation. And I could not source any organic dried Pinot or Sangiovese grapes, not even Merlot. Not anywhere. Period.

After sitting in a pool of defeat for a bit, I realized that nothing would happen if I didn't set a more determined, positive tone for expanding my line. I mustered a new feeling toward those limitations; I decided they just needed to be shown who was boss. First, I would find out what big mouth-filling flavors were available and then I would turn my imagination loose on those. I called the flavor houses but got some more wind sucked out of my sails. I was told, "This flavor is only available by the barrel" and "That flavor isn't shelf stable past four months" and "That flavor is being discontinued for lack of interest." When I asked them to create custom extractions for me, I was told I'd have to buy tens of thousands of dollars' worth to justify the development costs.

"Organics are just getting started," the suppliers told me. "We're still working some kinks out. And the demand is just not there. It's a trend we aren't sure we should be investing in yet."

I pulled myself together and went to the warehouse to take stock. I had roses, rose oil, lemon myrtle, licorice, three types of green tea (sencha, jasmine, and young hyson), four types of black tea (Darjeeling, Assam, Nilgiri, and Ceylon), and Rooibos (the bark of the South African red bush). I would have loved to count chamomile among the options, but all of the organic crops had been plagued with red beetles that year, which unfortunately had hatched at the most inopportune time (like on the desk of a Very Important Buyer).

I had a range of maybe ten ingredients from which to make a mouthwatering line of teas. I had to stick by my standard of organics, especially after what I'd sacrificed defending them, but I was starting to see the writing on the wall: Zhena's Gypsy Tea—Organically Boooooooring.

Wait! Zhena's *Gypsy* Tea. Gypsies wrote the book on living large within limitations. Grandma Maria had taught me about tea and passed on to me the secrets of our Gypsy heritage. Without ever traveling farther than a few blocks from her kitchen, our almighty matriarch combined the ingredients she had at hand into an infinite array of belly-pleasing meals, healing brews, and even some magical elixirs. If I could tap the spice, fervor, and resourcefulness of my grandma and her Gypsy ancestry, couldn't I create a line of teas that would turn nonbelievers into zealots for the natural taste of organic ingredients?

I closed up the warehouse, drove home, and ransacked my kitchen. I had the ingredients for chai—black tea and spices. I thought of all the teas I'd ever made in my own kitchen for curing or comforting friends. One tea I had created combined lavender petals, lavender oil, and licorice for a friend with chronic fatigue syndrome. The result, an intoxicating serum brewed pinkish-red and tasting like a French perfumery smelled, helped her feel better physically and mentally. Any of my one-off "friend blends" were candidates for inclusion in a gourmet lineup.

Hmm. Lavender oil.

In my bedroom, essential oils that I had made were arranged prettily on a painted tray. I blended these perfumes partially in order to maintain my sanity; the act of creating them was therapeutic in itself. But I hadn't thought to tap them for my tea recipes. Lilac, jasmine, lemon, ginger, cinnamon . . . I grabbed the tray and carried it to the kitchen. Then I went out to see what I had in the yard.

There, staring at me accusingly, was my peach tree—its branches straining under the weight of the fruit. I'd been so busy looking for flavors that I hadn't had time to pick the peaches. I filled my skirt with the fragrant fur-covered fruit and ran back to the house, noting the clusters of low-growing chocolate-mint that, until this moment, I'd regarded as an overgrown, invasive nuisance. Oh, and the lemon and orange trees! "I'll be back for you guys!" I shouted over my shoulder, thinking of all the things I could do with citrus peel.

I couldn't wait to try ginger oil with the peaches. Ginger chunks would be good, too. I found a wizened, thumb-shaped piece in the back of the crisper. Perfect! And already dried!

It was my first big flavor breakthrough. I dehydrated chunks of peaches in the repurposed food dehydrator I had acquired when I thought I would become a proper raw foodist. The dried peaches were extra potent. I cut them into pieces and added them to the bright red-toned black tea base blended from various Ceylon and Indian orange pekoes. Those simple ingredients made magic on the palate.

My optimism was recharged by this success, and my imagination started working overtime. Suddenly, inspiring and usable ingredients were everywhere, and blend ideas were waking me up in the middle of the night.

Over the next few months, I busied myself in my kitchen with a gram scale, oil droppers, professional porcelain tea-tasting sets, and my recipe journal. I wrote out hundreds of potential combinations. I had limited myself to using rose essential oil in Gypsy Love, but as I extended my research, I found that most of my homemade essential oils could be ingested in small quantities and even had health benefits. Essential oils were markedly stronger aromatically than flavorings but were barely detectable on the palate and didn't interfere with the taste of the tea. This unique method of blending would allow the tea drinker to smell the essential oil yet fully taste the tea leaves themselves. Essential oils changed the flavored tea paradigm. Through much trial and error, I discovered synergistic combinations to use in my product line and then named the blends: Gypsy Daydreaming was a lilac-scented sencha green tea, Gypsy Meditation was a vanilla-sandalwood-scented black tea with hawthorn and elderberries, Gypsy King was a cardamom-mint-scented Assam black tea with a hint of pine-smoked yerba mate, Gypsy Valentine was repurposed Gypsy Love with added vanilla extract and ginger pieces, Gypsy Afternoon carried the warm scent of cinnamon oil, dried orange peel, and chocolate nibs on a Darjeeling black tea base. Gypsy Zest was lively—Rooibos bark scented with lemon peels, lavender blossoms, and a drop of sage essential oil. This became Sage's own favorite, which he drank from his sippy cup.

By loving what I had, rather than focusing on what I lacked, I created a healing, flavor-rich, highly personal, and totally chemical-free line of teas. When my first price list went out to cafés, spas, and hotels, I had almost thirty blends because I had become skilled in recombining a few ingredients in many ways. Although I couldn't cook a gourmet meal out of three random ingredients like great chefs can, I could blend simple teas into tantalizing combinations. Discovering my own resourcefulness filled me again with enthusiasm.

Over the next few years, consumers' demand for organics increased, as did the availability of more affordable, flavorful ingredients in the amounts I needed. More tea growers converted to chemical-free production, and new technologies allowed organic extracts to fill the cup with an aroma of the fruits they were extracted from—without propylene glycol or any other poisonous "carrying agents." Nonetheless, I will always be grateful that I'd had to work with limited options at first because they made me expand my capabilities, which expanded my mind. As my aptitude grew, so did my business. Circumstances demanded that I create recipes within my standards and outside the supply chain of traditional, commercially available ingredients. Feeling hemmed in forced me to tap a new method of tea blending, creating a niche for myself in a saturated market. I rooted deep in my history with tea, my family heritage, enduring friendships, love of perfuming, and my desire to heal others. As a result, that original line was inventive and personal, and it created something new. It had its own rhythm and tone, leading the way for all of the blends that followed.

Blend What You've Got

*Mantra of the Cup: Limits fall away as soon as I learn
to thrive within them.*

Limits are like training wheels for your soul. They force you to learn to ride with less chance of a wipeout. Conventional wisdom dictates that more is always better and limitations always bad, but too many options can dilute the imagination. Great inspiration can come from being hemmed in by low funds, high standards, too many rules, or a seeming lack of choices. Obstacles force us inward into important resources that we might not otherwise discover. This can lead you into the land of loving what you have, which turns into cultivating your sight for opportunities.

Limits are like guardrails carefully lining the road leading to your dream. They are the universe's way of making sure you don't drive off a cliff when speeding toward your peak potential. Limitations also enhance creativity, help you discover your niche, make you an expert in a field, and help you define your life's purpose. Instead of beating your head against limits, examine them for any latent messages that lie dormant within them. Although they may appear daunting, they are rarely what they seem. They're always a calling card from our potential, asking us to tap into the great spirit of resourcefulness within our hearts.

My friend Susan cofounded One Kings Lane, a flourishing and successful website for home décor and furnishings. While most other flash-sale sites sell every category—clothes, shoes, travel, kids' toys, food, you name it, Susan and her team have kept primarily to home goods—a conscious, strategic limit that has given the market a clear and concise idea of their brand. By "limiting" their offerings, perfecting their niche, going deep within their chosen expertise, and clearly defining their promise to the world, they've had astronomical success—to the tune of hundreds of millions in annual sales.

Susan travels the world curating handmade art and décor, and she has discovered that the limited inventory inspires her customers to make the leap quickly and buy a one-of-a-kind or limited edition objects without hesitation. Although limiting your offerings is standard advice from branding and marketing experts, few companies have the discipline to carry out this strategy.

Limits instill in us a pressure to perform. As you look for your niche, you can find and stimulate your talents. Limiting your blog post to five hundred words makes you choose the best five hundred words. Using a budget requires you to maximize each cent. Counting calories makes each one count in the most delicious way. Decorating a small room inspires you to create expansive beauty out of an otherwise confining space.

Play with your limits, don't fear them. They come and go. Once, I wanted to hire a big, exciting New York City branding firm to help me clarify and float my brand in the sea of tea companies out in the world. But when I looked at my budget, I realized there wasn't any chance I could afford to retain them. I was sad, but then I decided to do a friends-and-family branding party instead. We got together, tasted each tea blend, and then wrote the words that came to mind as we sipped. This resulted in a wall taped top to bottom with index cards filled with poetic, defining attributes of our products, packaging, and essence. These descriptive words ended up becoming the basis of our mission statement, tagline, website, brochures, catalogs, displays, socially responsible manifesto, packaging copy, all of which eventually won branding and design accolades in magazines like *Brandweek*. Instead of spending $15,000 for a half-day session in New York City, it cost me five tins of tea, some wine, and a pizza, totaling $55.

Where are you feeling the pinch of limitation? Do you react by complaining, procrastinating, or going blank? We all do this at times, but the trick is to repeatedly remind yourself that everyone comes up against limits, but excavating them for their hidden treasure is the task at hand. How you respond to your momentary limit defines your long-term character. By confronting a limit head-on, you meet your most valuable internal resources. Exploring your limits like a curious traveler provides you with your map to shine the destiny that is yours alone.

Limitations demand that you become an alchemist and get really creative with the ingredients you've got on hand. Remind yourself to explore your limits: trace them with your finger, hike over them with big boots, and dance with them until they whisper their secrets. This will help you define your dream. Paradoxically, working with limitations makes your dream more accessible. Each limit is simply the medium through which your incomparable art is formed.

Now it's your turn to explore and play on your hidden opportunities and potentialities within the limitations in your life. Here's an exercise I use when I've lost sight of my choices and feel hemmed in.

Exercise: Mapping Limits, Making Opportunity

In this exercise, you won't focus on all that you aren't or don't have. You will focus on mapping all that you are and do have. You will use your limits as a launching pad for inspiration. Tapping the intangibles of your business, relationship, or job can offer you new vantage points for transmuting a present lack of resources into a map for future abundance.

Once, I made business cards for the tea company because I didn't have the money to print fancy brochures. I looked at the tiny template from the printer and wondered how I could turn such a small, informational product into a marketing machine. Then I got an idea. On a piece of paper, I wrote out all the positive, meaningful things our products and company stood for, the attributes that our tea and company aspired to embody. This list read: superior, fair trade, organic, natural, healthy, environmentally sound, socially conscious, well-being, holistic, quality, stewardship, artisanal, handcrafted, uncommon, innovative, pure, expertly blended, rigorous standards, uncompromising principles, prized, opulent, exuberant, luxurious, passionate, unadulterated, and committed. I typed everything without spaces and filled the back of the little business card with these big words. We were a small company, but when I handed my card to people, they could see that we stood for big things and had substantial dreams. That two-inch piece of paper became a calling card for our greatest good, and a reminder of our values each time we handed one to somebody.

You can do this for yourself, for a limit or a situation you are dealing with. Here's a way to map a limit in order to root out its opportunity.

1. Grab a pen, paper (or journal), and a digital timer. Find a quiet place to sit.

2. Get into a comfortable position and take five slow breaths deeply into your belly. This centers your energy and allows your creativity to flow.

3. Write down a limitation that you are struggling with or feel has been holding you back.

4. Set your digital timer for three minutes. Write all the positive attributes that this limit has helped you develop. Think about how this limit has potentially helped you to develop new skills, more positive facets of your character, or more creative solutions. Write without lifting your pen for the whole three minutes.

5. When the timer goes off, finish what you are writing, then look at the list.

When you feel yourself coming up against the limit again, review your list of all that you have developed as a result of this limitation. Focusing on this will help you transcend any feelings of being trapped and help you gain understanding. Use the list as a reminder if you get frustrated. Use it to help you gain perspective. These positive results and traits are the reason that limit has been in place: it's a gatekeeper, a teacher. As you reflect on all the personal growth that has come from it, you may notice it falling away.

> When you are inspired by some great purpose,
> some extraordinary project, all your thoughts break
> their bonds: Your mind transcends limitations, your
> consciousness expands in every direction, and you
> find yourself in a new, great, and wonderful world.
> Dormant forces, faculties, and talents become alive,
> and you discover yourself to be a greater person by far
> than you ever dreamed yourself to be.
>
> —PATANJALI,
> *founder of yoga, author of the Yoga Sutras*

9

Collaborate to Be Great

A Cup of Classic Twists

Alone we can do so little;
together we can do so much.

—HELEN KELLER

Inspiration: Raspberry Earl Grey tea. Sicilian Bergamot oranges convey Mediterranean sunshine and banter with the heart note of softly sweet raspberries in their perfect state of ripeness. The black teas used in this blend are a collaboration of greatness, growing in a perfect state of harmony with organic soil, light monsoon rains, and clean, clear mountain air. In the blue mountains of southern India's pristine Nilgiri range and in Sri Lanka's high country, the leaves grow on ridges that appear to float above Haputale's magical wildlife preserve. This blend harmonizes an adventure in flavor, a combination of old ideas (Earl Grey) and new additions (raspberries) with sustainability (organic, fair-trade-certified black tea).

While I am extremely proud of this tea, it was not my idea.

Back when this blend was born, I was a solo flyer and all about authenticity. If my name was on it, dammit, it had to originate with me. I felt that if an idea wasn't mine alone, it would be inauthentic to use it in my product line—because, after all, the product line bore my name. It wasn't just my scruples that kept me from using other people's ideas. I was a single mom, hustling to sell enough tea to pay the rent and cover the new bills that were a by-product of my company's recent growth spurt. I had little time to consider feedback because I was so busy with Sage and the business. Looking back, I must have come off as downright defensive, but not because I didn't want others to offer their insights. I was just too tired to accept them. And I rarely got enough sleep because my mind was always racing around what needed to get done next.

You probably know that feeling—when you're stressed, you can't make space for even the most well-intentioned opinions about what you "should" do with your business or your life. When you've started a business, like when you're pregnant, everyone feels at liberty to offer his or her unsolicited opinion about what you should be doing instead of what you actually are doing.

I had formulated a new line of aromatherapy teas, and now it was time to get the products into more hands and cups. That meant personally presenting the tea in different venues and explaining their distinctive qualities to each potential new customer. So I manned booths at local events like Ojai Day and the Peddlers' Fair, held tastings, and hosted a slew of Gypsy Tea

Parties. I even schlepped big pots of hot tea to an abandoned farm after a solstice festival to serve late-night revelers and campers.

I signed up for events, paid the concession fee, and showed up extra early with my little table, a silky tablecloth, my poster board logo, and hand-packed corsage bags of tea that I had blended the night before. I tied each pouch with a little raffia bow, stuck on a label, and handwrote the name of the blend in the blank space under the company name. I also wrote Grandma Maria's Gypsy sayings on tiny scrolls and tucked the fortunes inside the bags.

Usually, I had one-year-old Sage with me, so I had to make the absolute most of my time out in public. He was a baby time bomb, and I had to sell-sell-sell before he would need a diaper change, to nurse, or get fed up with being confined to the pack on my back and throw a mood-curdling fit, clawing at my hair or earrings.

Planning ahead to a day when my mother would be able to watch Sage, I set up a tasting at one of the prestigious local spas. It had been hard to get permission to present there. I spent a week preparing for it so that I would give the women the best tea experience ever.

I was the youngest person there, which made me feel extra nervous. The women had come to this health spa from all over the country to lose weight and get in shape. Since tea has no calories, therapeutic teas seemed perfect to introduce to people in a rejuvenating spa setting. Of course, I hoped the women would love them enough to buy a lot and keep me in business.

I served tea to about thirty women, waxing poetic about the various types of leaves, the difference among natural, organic, and artificial flavors, the nuances of essential oils when blended into the leaves, and the faraway terroirs of the teas. I romanticized the exotic tea fields and shared what I knew of fair trade and its positive effects on the workers. When describing teas, I would go into an inspired spiel, full of lush descriptions and terms from tasting notes. As I was pontificating about all the sensual details of my new signature aromatherapeutic blends, a woman raised her hand and interrupted me.

"What's the difference between this tea and Lipton?" she challenged.

This was not the reception I had hoped for. I replied, "I source only organic teas and I use only certified organic essential oils. I blend unusual combinations of ingredients you cannot find anywhere else, and the names of the teas reflect my grandmother's heritage as a Gypsy." I wanted to say, "And I am not a $500 million company, but starting up a new business and a new way of doing business."

"Yeah," she said and shrugged. "None of that means I would change from Lipton to your tea. It's way too complex." She looked around at the other women, and they nodded. I was crushed. All of the researching, writing, rehearsing, and preparation hadn't equipped me for this. I felt defensive, but I understood that being defensive would be terrible for sales, so I breathed and tried to smile as she continued.

"You should do something like take simple, old-style tea and add something new to it—like a twist," she said.

I wasn't expecting to receive a marketing lesson at this event, but I had actually had a good night's sleep, so I could take it in. I asked, "What kind of twist?"

"Like putting fruit with Earl Grey, berries, stuff like that. Raspberries maybe. Make it really interesting but also recognizable to old gals like me." She sat back in her chair and the other women nodded.

"Thank you," I said. "I'll consider it." Proud of myself for handling the exchange with some grace and grateful that it was over so quickly, I finished my lecture without further incident.

Afterward, all the women got up and looked at my pretty display of teas in their shiny little corsage bags with bows. But the names—Gypsy Daydreaming, Gypsy Afternoon, and Gypsy Valentine—seemed to confuse them. I explained each blend thoroughly—the flavors, the properties, the inspiration, how different aromatherapy oils worked to produce mood-enhancing benefits. But in the end, they only bought one or two. I didn't understand. Where was the excitement that I was used to getting from my friends and the Ojai community? Maybe it was because these women weren't hipsters who liked the esoteric Gypsy names but strangers who were not familiar with my story or quirky ideas. These women were from different states and would be buying tea in other parts of the country, in grocery stores where I would not be standing in the aisle explaining each obscure name and hidden health benefit. I bit my lip with the realization that my niche, my tea, wasn't translating to anyone outside my immediate circle of sympathetic buddies or my small geographic zone. A wave of panic came over me.

The woman who had mentioned adding raspberries to the tea walked up to me and whispered in my ear, "See, if you had raspberry Earl Grey, I bet they'd all buy it."

I nodded, feeling a little hurt. Did she have to rub it in? I bristled inwardly, thinking to myself, "You try building a tea company by yourself, with a toddler in tow, on no sleep."

But then I looked around at these women, most of whom were my mother's age or older, and realized many of them had a completely different relationship with tea—a relationship formed in a time when it was Lipton or nothing. This woman had allowed me to benefit from her perspective, one I could not come to by "flying solo." Her perspective would open up a whole new customer base for me.

I touched the woman's arm. "Thank you for your idea. It's a great one, and I'm going to try it as soon as I get home."

She smiled. "You know, in all my years of life and business, I have found that it's not until you collaborate that you can be great."

As I packed my poster board sign and samples back into the trunk of my little car, I was already thinking about how to blend that flavor, what percentages I would need and which base tea would best showcase the complexity of this sweet and citrusy flavor profile.

When I got home, I rummaged through my collection of oils and found a small vial of Sicilian Bergamot. I bought a packet of freeze-dried raspberries at the health food store and went about blending the oil, the berries, and the black tea together. The scent lifted my mood and energized me. I found myself running back to my kitchen to smell the tea as the essential oil dried on the leaves and berries. It got better each time.

At my next tea-tasting event, Raspberry Earl Grey was a raving success. I didn't have to explain it to people. The name sold it practically all by itself. It was effortless.

Collaborate to Be Great

Mantra of the Cup: Collaboration allows me to see the answers to my questions through another's eyes.

Dreams and ideas are born within us, from our spirits. Our minds attempt to translate them to the world, and then reality or feedback tempers them into being. To make dreams real in the material world, we have to translate them into a language others can understand. This takes collaboration.

How are you at taking feedback? Do you love it? Hate it? Simply tolerate it in order to keep the peace? For people with big personalities and big ideas, letting go of the wheel might be uncomfortable at first, but collaboration is an art worth learning and refining. It gets easier and more fun with time. The wisdom I gained from the woman at the spa transformed my life, teaching me that feedback could help me clarify my creativity for the marketplace, which would then actually accept it more widely and with less effort on my part.

If you've ever tried to coparent, cochair, be a partner on a project, or take constructive criticism, then you know that collaboration takes two or more willing participants. It's not always easy or harmonious, but the result is almost always greater than the sum of its parts. TV writers exemplify collaborating. They write alone at first, then do their rewrites in a group. For instance, The Daily Show with Jon Stewart has more than twelve writers and eight producers working in tandem on each episode. Together, they write for up to ten hours a day. The head writer, Steve Bodow, once said, "In the writing room during rewrites, a writer can spit out five or six funny jokes in five to ten minutes. It's what the hive-mind can do."

Collaborating doesn't come naturally to those of us taught to be independent and self-possessed. Many women are taught not to rely on others, so the idea of collaborating or "handing off your baby" can be scary. But once you try it, you're likely to find more success than if you had struggled alone.

As I moved through the business world, I realized that my success relied on contributions from farmers, tea pluckers, tea factory workers, estate managers, freight forwarders, packaging designers, manufacturers, essential oil distillers, importers, organic certifiers, fair-trade auditors, grocery store buyers, restaurant distributors, chefs, retailers, and consumers. I concluded that the solo-preneuer cannot successfully exist in my chosen field. I had to engage, build, and trust a highly collaborative tribe of talented people to help me. I concluded that the idea of self-made is a myth. Taking initiative and creating something took courage, but I couldn't fulfill my idea's potential without the efforts of others. If it takes a village to raise a child, it takes a metropolis to raise a child and a business.

As my company grew, I collaborated with retailers on successful marketing strategies, having belly dancers in stores to promote the products, which made us a memorable (to say the least) company. I held tastings around the country and received more flavor ideas from which great new blends were born—and people bought the new blends because they had had a hand in creating them.

Soliciting feedback can be as easy as asking simple questions of a friend: "How do these look on me? How does this line read? Do you think it needs more salt?" Requesting collaboration can help you with life's bigger issues, too. "Do you think I am making the right decision? Am I a good manager? How can I be a better parent?"

Even when your name is on a product, collaboration is not only okay—it presents an opportunity to grow. An outside opinion may show you a turning point to greatness, or it could become your saving grace if you're about to make a mistake. You needn't take every single idea to heart, but by being willing to collaborate, you'll be ready when a game-changing idea comes along.

Recently, I attended Scott Coady's Art of Leadership Mastery program, a seven-month course in collaborative, embodied leadership training initially developed for NASA, where Coady taught it for over a decade. It proved to me again the power of collaboration. In the course, Scott requires each attendee to commit to a Leadership Project, which is a personal goal the attendee previously thought was impossible for her to attain. Attendees divide into learning teams in which they attend weekly calls where they collaborate and hold one another accountable to do daily exercises, weekly readings, and take the necessary steps to complete their big learning project.

My project was to create a women's retreat called A Woman's Power, and not only did my team help me achieve the creation and facilitation of that amazing three-day event for forty women, but something unexpected happened in our weekly calls. Each week, a part of my soul bloomed in the light of my team's attention. Through sharing in these calls, and hearing my words and ideas reflected back to me, I realized that I wanted to create and grow a nonprofit as well as the women's retreat.

In each call, we'd take a few minutes to talk about our week and how we were doing. I heard myself say things that were clues to a larger message about what I really wanted for my life—and that was to focus on a greater program for the education of women and children in the tea fields. The synergy that was formed by the space we teammates all held for each other to talk gave us an enormous amount of insight into our deeper selves. Each call was like a psychological or emotional excavation. Together, we noticed obvious things about ourselves that had been sitting in plain view but had been hidden in our blind spots. I was surprised by what I uncovered about myself. It was a remarkable gift to see myself from others' points of view, and it helped me uncover a part of my destiny that had been latent.

So many little miracles were born of simply setting up a space for us to talk together once a week. One of my teammates decided to train for the Olympics and is doing so as the oldest woman to train and compete in Olympic rowing. Another teammate discovered a path within his music to aid patients with heart disease and is now teaching the power of music to nurses nationwide. Yet another teammate found that his love of writing children's books helped his teaching career and he ended up getting his dream job in a new school district. None of us could have predicted what we would learn about ourselves simply by committing to speak to each other and to hear what we said through the reflection and mirroring of our teammates.

When we open ourselves to collaborate, we get more than we expect or give individually. The gifts received in return for being open to possibility are varied and surprising. Uncovering greater truths that grow us into greater humans happens when we share, talk, and listen collectively. The universe speaks to us through the voices of others.

There is a saying, "We are the average of the five people

we spend the most time with." My learning team ensured the five people I spent a lot of time with were stellar at pointing out my strengths and helping to fortify my weaknesses. Besides the women's retreat I organized, where forty women collaborated and formed new partnerships, friendships, and products, I formed a nonprofit, Educate Her, Inc. I used the profits from the retreat to benefit the tea growers' children. This collaboration showed me it was possible to empower both women here in America and children in Sri Lanka—my team generously showed me the way.

Seeking out brilliant people to collaborate with is a brilliant way to ensure your average gets better every single day. Whenever you feel stuck, pick up the phone and start collaborating with a trusted friend or colleague.

Where can you go from solo flyer to collaboration machine in your life? Collaboration can be a sacred exchange of creativity if you allow it to be. When feelings of being stuck pervade you, open up your ideas for your personal or professional life to collaboration and feedback.

Exercise: Feedback Forum

For this exercise, you will take an idea or problem you are stuck on and a make a "playdate" with a friend, colleague, or mentor. Set a time to meet and ask your friend to bring something he or she could use help on, whether it's a song, website layout, blog, book idea, résumé, recipe, business plan—anything. Once you set the date, gather the items on which you need feedback to show your friend and have a couple notebooks ready for your meeting.

When the time arrives, follow these steps:

1. Share your idea with your partner and have her write down every single thought that comes to mind—or speak each one aloud as you take notes.

2. Brainstorm ideas back and forth about what she sees in your idea, and her ideas on how to improve it. Let her ask lots of questions, and if you feel nervous or defensive, breathe through the feelings.

3. Write down all her ideas, even those that do not immediately resonate with you. Record the feedback with an open mind and try not to edit the suggestions.

4. Next, share all of the things you need in order to make your idea come to life or the burden to be lifted. Whether it's money, volunteers, or a web designer, ask your friend to help you clarify concisely what you need. Make a list.

5. If this person cannot directly help you fulfill the needs, ask whom she knows who might be able to help. Make a list of resources.

6. Now you should have a list of ideas to improve your idea or achieve your goal, a list of what you need to accomplish these improvements or goal, and a list of resources to approach for help to do so.

7. Now it's your partner's turn to go through the same process with you. Be supportive and positive, and tap your inner wisdom for ideas to help your friend see all of the potentials in her idea. Watch her face and observe what she's most excited about and mirror back to her what you saw—what she is most enthusiastic about will be a clue to her motivations and potential success.

8. Set up other feedback forums for colleagues and friends, so that you can allow collaboration to shine. Set up a monthly, or even a weekly, forum, to ensure that you continue to receive support and support others in their dreams. Ultimately, spontaneous, highly creative ideas will spring from this ritual. Be prepared to be happily surprised.

As you navigate through the rest of your life, be open to collaboration. Other people and other people's ideas are often better than your own. Find a group of people who challenge and inspire you, spend a lot of time with them, and it will change your life.

—AMY POEHLER,
actress and comedian

10

Answer the Call

A Cup of Connections

Every calling is great when greatly pursued.

—OLIVER WENDELL HOLMES

Inspiration: Divine Tea, a hand-tied green tea that blooms like a bud unfolding into a flower when steeped. The worker chooses the newest, most tender leaves and buds, sifting through each one to ensure there are no blemishes. She steams each leaf in order to arrest the oxidation and preserve the delicate flavor, and carefully rolls the leaf in the palm of her hand. Then she carefully bundles together the soft, pliant leaves and carefully ties them with thin string to make a tight mushroom-shaped bud, concealing the string so that the bloom looks natural.

The artisan tea makers sit four or five to a table talking quietly in between long bouts of concentrated silence. As they tighten the string to seal the bud, their words seep into the leaves like messages in a bottle, their thoughts, ideas, worries, prayers, and conversation captured until the tea is steeped. The finished blossoms dry in mountain air for several hours, then the workers pack them carefully into small boxes for shipment. Divine Tea is air freighted instead of shipped across the Indian and Pacific Oceans in order to preserve its ethereal honey flavor.

My tea importer gave me my first small packet of Divine Tea for Christmas. Late one night, as I sat at my desk, I poured hot water over one of the buds and watched it unfurl. I turned off the computer and took the tea over to my altar to sit quietly and observe it. The golden color opened up like wisps of smoke in humid air. As I sipped the sweet liquor of the leaf, I could hear the message in the leaves. This time it had a sense of urgency.

The call I'd heard in my first crate of tea—to sell that crate and then a hundred more in order to be able to travel to meet the tea workers—had been quickly drowned out by day-to-day business. Three years passed before I realized I had far exceeded that one-hundred-crate goal. I now made enough money to pay rent and medical bills with a little extra for treats—a scented candle, a down pillow, cut flowers.

Sage and I were living in a beautiful little guesthouse and had our own rooms, although he still slept in mine in his little race-car-shaped bed at the foot of my own. Our landlady, a kind Japanese woman named Masako who wore kimono, nurtured us as if we were her own. She often left Japanese tea on my doorstep along with little gifts for Sage—clothes, shoes, coloring books, cookies. I had so much to be grateful for. Sage and I left every morning for the office at 7, and returned home after 7 each night, but long hours were a tiny price to pay for the dignity and independence the company had given me.

My days were spent monitoring Sage's health, increasing tea sales, hiring a small team of employees (which I called my tribe), putting tea in tea bags, designing new packaging, navigating new distribution channels, attending trade shows, managing a budget, scheduling advertising, and getting certified as a woman-owned enterprise, which allowed us to avoid having to pay for expensive shelf space in stores that the big companies controlled. It all felt so upwardly mobile and *optimistic*, even though we were always a decimal point from shuttering our doors. Our margins were perpetually razor thin.

A lot of people were counting on me to succeed and, as I continued to bury myself in the business of tea, their hope redeemed me. My past sins were erased. I was a respectable businesswoman now. I had paid off my share of Sage's first two operations. I didn't have to beg my parents or brothers for money anymore or for them drive the two hours to babysit Sage while I worked my weekend jobs. I was a tea maker, an entrepreneur, an independent woman, and author of my destiny.

Although things were going my way, I knew that with one misstep, I could lose it all. Sales were growing but not astronomically. I had been able to raise more capital from my angel investors to cover the highs and lows of seasonal sales. While the tribe and I worked tirelessly through slow seasons, I worried that we weren't making the milestones and progress in my business plan. I was so grateful for our momentum, yet in quiet moments, my old fears of being back in dire circumstances surfaced.

I shook like a leaf every time I saw the county hospital. One day, I heard on NPR News that the Bush administration had cut the Healthy Kids, Healthy Families program for children with health problems who couldn't afford insurance. This was the very program that had saved Sage's life. I pulled over and cried for the babies who wouldn't be given care.

Although I felt like I had pushed past my personal glass ceiling of poverty and dependence, it was an anxious time. On the one hand, I had a beautiful product line of delicious teas and bountiful opportunities, but on the other hand, I had a very pronounced feeling of unease in my core, as if a piece of my soul were missing.

Each time I felt the powerful spiritual draw to visit and meet the people at the source of my teas, I suppressed it as a selfish, irresponsible impulse. Taking off for India sounded like something the old impetuous, premotherhood me would have done—not the one who brought home the (veggie) bacon, got Sage to school, and had a *tribe.*

Then one day I met with a representative from the nonprofit TransFair (now called Fair Trade USA), which advocates fair trade and recruits businesses to adhere to fair-trade practices. He showed me pictures of tea workers and statistics about them: infant mortality rates as high as 50 percent in some estates, little or no access to doctors, electricity, or running water. A female tea picker has to support four or more dependents on less than $2 a day, often as the sole breadwinner, yet she has no medical care, no maternity leave, no child care, and no place to go after retirement. When exposed to pesticides, she is ten times more likely than tea workers in organic fields to get cancer.

Fair trade is popular in Europe but less so in the United States, and without a mass increase in fair-trade tea sales volumes, most of these women will continue to suffer. Tea is grown primarily in India, Sri Lanka, China, and Africa. It's considered a commodity just like coffee and corn. Commodities are traded as numbers and hedged by financial institutions. When a tea estate harvest is ready to be sold, it goes through the auction system. First, a tea taster puts a price on it; then it goes up for bid. Many factors dictate the price the tea can fetch for the tea grower: flavor, weather, other people's budgets, financial markets, demand, and, if they are lucky, relationships. A government that subsidizes tea drives down the price for all competing teas.

Tea is such an artful, meditative beverage, the second-most-drunk liquid in the world next to water. The making of tea seemed so elegant, poetic, idyllic, but the markets, the model of trading it, removed any humanity from the equation. The business of it could be cruel. How did all of the human effort boil down to a number? Tea estate workers are referred to simply as "labor"; the health of the plant and soil is "yield." From there it's price per kilo, price per lot, and it becomes a penny business in which the price is taken out of the hands of those who actually do the work to grow it.

I figured the only way to break this cycle was to build life-long relationships with the people who grow the tea itself, to buy it before it goes to auction, to give the tea estate manager a number, a projection for the years to come, so he can count on it and plan around it. This couldn't be done in a quarterly return business model, where the cheapest tea makes the best financial results for the tea brand buying it up. It had to be a long-term, compassionate, human, unified, transparent business model. I didn't want cold transaction-based business to run my supply chain—it had to be integrated, like a family. If it was going to feel authentic, it had to embody compassion. I aspired for there to be love in each transaction. If the "old-school" plantation-owning men had put this system in place, I as a "new-school" woman resolved to buck it.

I wouldn't allow our company to perpetuate poverty for our own profits. The picture of the tea gardens shown by the representative of TransFair was not the bright and beautiful vision I had seen in my first crate of tea. If our company went fair trade, we would pay a premium directly to the tea workers so that they could organize, vote, use the money for what they needed: schools, clean water, electricity, and health care. Fair trade bypassed auctions and managers to create human-to-human contact. The health care was especially important for me. To think that I had started my company to pay for Sage's surgeries but that the workers who had made that possible didn't have health care haunted me. We had to cultivate safety and compassion for those making it possible for us to sell tea.

Fair trade had to become the other half of our mission, along with organic certification. We were taking care of the earth and soil but needed to consider the *people*. Having almost lost my newborn, I felt connected to the tea workers and their children. I signed on without hesitation to become entirely fair-trade certified.

I presented my employees with the new information at the next tribal meeting. "This guarantees worker rights to vote, unionize, receive health care, maternity leave, fair wages, education, and that there is no child labor." They were enthusiastic and their motivation rose over the next few months without any effort on my part—we were in our small way saving the world. Besides doing the added paperwork, we set aside the premium money for the workers; at the time it was a euro per kilo—approximately $1.40.

Those fair-trade premium payments added up. We paid them each quarter and had to cut marketing to compensate. We could no longer pay for Gypsy Tea Parties or in-store tastings and had to put off printing catalogs. It was a small price to pay. I couldn't wait any longer to go to the fields. I was betting my whole life on this company and its mission. Now I had a responsibility to my customers, employees, investors, and vendors to seek and find the truth of our purpose for them.

"There are always going to be reasons to deny a call," my meditation teacher, Jagat Joti, said. "Go learn what's calling. Leave the rest to God."

With my angel investors' blessing and their added funds, I was able to put together the budget to go to Sri Lanka. I bought a plane ticket and slept with it under my pillow. I sent letters to the tea growers, hoping they would get them and know I was coming. I had never been away from Sage for more than a couple days and I had never been so far away from home. I feared getting lost and not being able to find my way back to him.

I explained to Sage every day for a month that I was going away for a week. He just said, "Okay, Mommy," and went about playing. To this day he doesn't remember my being away that first time, but had I not gone, I would.

There were no direct flights to Sri Lanka, so I had to fly through New Delhi. The layover was almost two days, and at the urging of my mentor and meditation teacher, I planned to take the Shatabdi Express train up to the Golden Temple in Amritsar, a sacred site for Sikhs. The philosophy of Sikhism resonated with my Christian upbringing: There is one God and we can reach God through acts of service to others.

"You'll never be the same," he said.

"I hope so," I replied.

Even though I worried about Sage and the tea company, after

flying over the International Date Line for the first time, I also felt elated and inspired. I was on a plane to the other side of the world! While in the air, I wrote down dozens of questions to ask the tea estate managers, penned a list of wishes for the next year of my life (I'd be at the Golden Temple for my birthday), and even listed the traits of a soul mate I hoped for. I prayed that the week would transform me. In preparation for visiting the Golden Temple, I read the teachings of Guru Nanak, founder of the Sikh religion.

I landed in the middle of the night and the hot, humid air was hard to breathe. Escorted out of the airport and driven through the capital city's embassy row, I was dropped at the Taj Hotel on Mansingh Road. I'd never stayed in a hotel nicer than a Best Western, so I marveled at the palatial lobby—marble and mahogany—and a staff so attentive I felt a little embarrassed by their kindnesses. The room cost less than $90 a night, but in contrast to the shanties I had seen along the drive, it was an obscene display of wealth and luxury.

The next morning at the train station, I played with some children and wrote out the English alphabet for them on a piece of paper. A little girl in stained boy's clothing eagerly traced the letters with her finger and repeated the sounds as I made them. She smiled as I praised her. I bought the little band of children samosas and juice from a street vendor and gave them a handful of rupees. They ate quickly and stuffed the rupees into their pockets. One little boy fed his samosa to a tiny puppy hidden in his coat. As the train pulled up, my heart felt like it would burst. I didn't want to leave them there, alone. Just then a man walked up to me and said, "Madam, these children used to work in the factories down the way, but new laws prohibit child labor."

"That's a great thing," I said.

"Well, maybe so, but their parents depended on them to work and eat at the factory. Now they live at the station."

"Why aren't they in school?"

"School costs a lot here, it's not free. I didn't mean to upset you, I just wanted to thank you for treating them with kindness."

I couldn't respond. The station roared with engine noise and I leaned down and kissed the little girl's cheek. I gave her the rupees that were left in my pouch. The train sounded its departure and the man urged me to get on board. "Madam, they like it here, they get to have all sorts of adventures and mischief. They could go home if they really wanted to."

The whole train ride, I wrestled with what I just learned. Child labor ensured the kids would be fed? School wasn't free? Parents needed them to work so they could eat? These realities stabbed holes in my ideals.

The man from the station found me and lightly tapped my shoulder.

"Excuse me, Madam. I'm sorry to have upset you, it was not my intention. It's unfortunate about so many of the children, but it's just the current reality. When certain laws take place, they do not consider all of the small details, the context. Children and people fall through the cracks. Reform is not without its price."

That little girl was Sage's age, living alone in a train station with a group of preschool- and grade-school-age kids. I ached to be back home with Sage, feeding him, holding him, teaching him the alphabet. I hated what I now knew and couldn't help but feel responsible. A few samosas, some juice, and a pittance of rupees would not change the lives of the kids I'd just met. But I hoped fair trade was real and that it would make me part of the solution, not the problem.

A rickshaw from the train station dropped me in front of the Golden Temple, but the crowds and chaos kept me from moving my feet. The poverty outside the temple walls battered me. Beggars with severe physical deformities sat in the street with outstretched palms. Young women with matted hair approached me, searching my face for compassion and my hands for alms. I stood in a puddle in the street looking for a way into the temple, bewildered.

A massive line of people stood waiting as Sikhs spooned dal into bowls and handed them to each person. Other Sikhs poured chai into cups and offered them, smiling radiantly. I walked over and stood close enough to smell the savory dal and spicy tea, remembering my meditation teacher repeating his guru's words, "In your commitment is your essence of your flow of spirit. In your commitment you know who you are. Without commitment, you do not know who you are."

This trip was already challenging my commitment. My fear of poverty was illuminated in Technicolor here. Everything I was scared of was laid before me. Yet the servers looked happily on the endless line of people in need as they shared the food and tea. The Sikhs' loving-kindness inspired me, and I realized that my teacher had sent me here for more than meditation—it was to grow past my own fears, and to learn gratitude. Each hand reached out to receive a single serving of sustenance and was filled. And most everyone was smiling. I remembered a quote by one of the Sikh gurus, "The greatest comforts and lasting peace are obtained when one eradicates selfishness from within."

I walked up to one of the men serving tea and asked him, "Do you do this every day?"

"Yes, Madam. Guru Nanak started this daily practice to feed and nourish all people—rich or poor, all social castes and any religion—to build solidarity and show that all humans are equal. From kings to untouchables—people are one."

He handed me a small cup of milky tea.

"We give meals to tens of thousands of people a day, and no matter how many we serve, there is always enough food. That is the power of God."

I sat on the ground next to a group of women. Sipping the tea, I reflected on the chaotic scene and how calmly the Sikhs served, treating all people with kindness and dignity. All servings of dal were given for the sake of giving, not giving for the sake of saving.

This could have been what the man on the train meant—when giving, do so with a heart of compassion for the people, with grace, not in order to be a hero. Especially when giving from afar. Giving for others' sakes looked much different from giving to make oneself feel better. My motivations for fair trade had to come from a place of giving for the sake of giving, knowing we are all one in the eyes of God. I couldn't do it because I was still scared of poverty, felt guilty, or wanted to feel better about myself. I had to do it without being attached to the outcome. I was being asked to learn grace.

When we bury or run from our fears, we risk being destroyed by them. Here, my fear was everywhere, and suddenly it was nowhere. My call to action had to be tin by tin, cup by cup, one serving at a time, which would eventually become many. It had to be done daily, like the Sikhs who stood outside the temple walls without needing recognition or credit for their *seva* (service). The rewards were not in the results but in the act of giving equally to all people, tirelessly. If I'm scared of poverty, I must help others through theirs. The only way to heal your own life is to offer it to others.

I made my way into the temple grounds, where pilgrims were dipping into the holy waters that surrounded the shimmering golden temple. I climbed to the top floor of the temple and looked out over the ancient, sacred grounds. Devotees humbly washed the temple floors with fresh milk, on hands and knees. I took a tin of tea from my backpack and offered a pinch of it back to the sacred Ganges water that had helped it grow.

The message was clear: Give for the sake of honoring all life as sacred. This was the giving that I was to witness and learn before my trip to the tea fields.

I sat and meditated for a few hours before making my way back outside. The Sikhs were still tirelessly serving food and tea, honoring each person through a heart of service.

That night at the train station, I looked for the children who lived there and spotted the little girl in boy's clothing. She and her small gang were standing next to a tall Australian couple, drinking juice with straws as the couple gave them postcards and sweets from their backpacks. The little girl and I caught each other's eyes and she smiled, waving at me like an old friend. She turned back to the tall foreigners and I boarded the train, feeling the emotions of loss and awe at once.

When I arrived back at the hotel in New Delhi, a striking woman, dressed in all black, was standing on the steps. At first I though she was a pop star. People approached her for her autograph and crowded around her while others simply stared. We caught each other's eyes and I was startled to see that she looked exactly like my aunt Lala. I felt compelled to approach her. No one looked like Lala, the darkest of my father's siblings and the most beautiful. High cheekbones and full lips, big elegant eyes and dark black hair—in her youth she had been a legend in my hometown. As I approached this woman, I noticed intricate tribal tattoos on her face. A silver ring in her nose bore ornate elaborate chains that sloped up her cheek, connecting to a moon-shaped hoop earring with red stones.

I overheard a woman saying, "Look, it's the Queen of the Gypsies."

I walked up to her and took her hands. "Excuse me, are you a *Gypsy*?"

She said proudly, "I am Sherma, the spokesperson for all the Gypsy tribes of India."

I couldn't believe it. I said, "I'm a Ukrainian Gypsy!"

"You are a Gypsy and you do not know who *I am*?"

"I have a company called Gypsy Tea . . . in *America*!"

"You cannot have such a thing without knowing me. You must come to Rishikesh to see the Gypsies with me. I am helping ensure my people, the Banjara, have the basics—water pumps, emergency kits . . ."

I was stunned. I had planned my trip solely around tea and fair trade, forgetting the other most important part of my life and company—my Gypsy heritage, which originated in outcast tribes from India more than a thousand years ago. How could I have planned a trip to the birthplace of my heritage without planning a trip to meet my people?

"I can't," I stammered. "I'm sorry, I have a flight in the morning to see the tea fields. But I'm doing the same kind of work as you are, just through my teas . . ."

A driver waved for her and she nodded to him. She said, "Here is my mobile number. I'll be here whenever you return. Remember, India is the birthplace of all Gypsies. It's our motherland." She looked at my face, examining my eyes, adding, "It's *your origin.*"

"Sherma, will you please bless my company?" I searched through my backpack frantically for the tea tin to give her.

"You do not need a blessing," she said as she walked toward the waiting car, "as long as you remember the magic of the land you came from and do not forget to honor our name."

I stood on the steps for some time reflecting on the miracles of the day. Never in all my life could I have predicted this encounter. Of all the steps, of all the hotels, it was here that I met Sherma. My heritage was an even greater source of honor and pride.

That night, I wrote the details of the day as best I could remember in my green velvet journal, while nestled in bed sipping fresh mint tea. My throat hurt from the thickly polluted air I had breathed all day; my eyes were swollen from crying as I prayed for Sage's health in a ceremony at the temple. I was surprised by a knock on the door. When I opened it, a few hotel staff members burst into song—singing "Happy Birthday" to me. They must have gotten the date from my passport when I checked in! They presented me with a beautiful chocolate cake that said, "Happy Birthday, Miss Zhena." A card on the tray said, "Welcome to India, Miss Zhena, and many happy returns to you." They all smiled as I thanked them.

My eyes welled up and my heart felt like it would burst from gratitude.

The many layers of India took my breath away. Dark, light, miracle, mundane. All the colors of soul and tribe, spirit and song resonated through me.

The next day I flew into Colombo, the capital of Sri Lanka. The landscape was tropical, the air moist and clean. It was so different from India. The owners of the tea estate I was there to visit had helped organize a car and driver for me and we dodged head-on collisions with huge buses, whole families riding on motorcycles, and swerving tuk-tuks. The one-lane road to the tea estate was washed out from the rain in several spots and the drive took almost eight hours. We stopped several times at my urging for tea at the roadside restaurants. At one stop, a man played the flute from high in a massive tree. He caught my eye and smiled, pointing to his tip jar on the edge of a wooden railing.

For the first time, I saw tea bushes, planted in perfect rows that stretched for miles, and stopped at least ten times to touch and photograph them. Huge waterfalls cut through the green lines of tea bushes in the distance, where I also saw tea pluckers hunching over the plants with big baskets on their backs, their colorful saris dotting the landscape like bright Christmas lights.

When we finally arrived in the Bio-Tea Project in Haputale, I was surprised to see a huge banner at the entrance gate that said WELCOME TO ZEENA, SPECIAL GUEST FROM USA! I felt so honored and humbled. We pulled into the driveway in front of the main office, where a row of women in matching peach-hued saris and at least fifty children stood in a half circle waving at me. The kids jumped up and down as I got out of the car and a man with wire-rimmed glasses approached and hugged me. He said, "Hello, Miss Zeena, I am Gnana, the manager here. Welcome. We are soooo very pleased to meet you, Miss Zeena. It is truly a very great honor, very wonderful indeed."

The children swarmed Gnana and me, and some of them shyly reached out to touch the fabric of my dress sleeve. They smiled up at me with sparkling eyes. Each of them had a red dot on her forehead. The girls had colorful, plastic flower barrettes in their shiny black hair. I sent a small prayer to the children in the train station of New Delhi, noticing the contrast between the two groups of children.

One of the women in a peach sari stepped out and placed a jasmine flower lei around my neck and lightly kissed me on both cheeks as she took my hands and looked deeply into my eyes. She said, "Thank you, Miss Zeena, for coming to us from so very far away. We are truly honored."

A child approached me carrying a tray with metal bowls and shyly motioned me to lean down while another child placed a finger in a silver bowl full of red powder. She gently placed the finger on my forehead and smiled at the result. She said, "Thank you, Miss Zeena for coming to see us."

A big mural on a building behind the crowd showed a little girl running in a garden. Above the picture were the words, "We are living in a happy and healthy environment, organic concept for social progress." Another saying was painted on a piece of wood on a fence to my left: "When love and skill work together, expect a miracle."

A big-eyed little girl pulled on my sleeve and said, "We are very pleased to meet you, Miss Zeena." Gnana patted her on the head and with a proud smile said, "This is Durga. She is a very good student and her mother is a tea plucker here."

A young woman kissed both of my cheeks, "I am Neesa, so nice to finally meet you. Miss Zeena, would you like to say a few words?" She handed me a bouquet of flowers and motioned for me to turn around and speak to the crowd. Through big, welling, happy tears, I said, "I have been dreaming of this day for years. I feel like I know you through the tea leaves I have been receiving and sharing with those in America. I feel very close to you. I feel like you are my family."

Gnana translated and the group clapped. Gnana then asked, "Zeena, we have heard your story, about how you built your company from nothing, and how you did so to save your son. Can you please share this story with our people?"

"Gnana, it's all in the past. I am more keen to hear your stories," I said.

"Please, Zeena, this story I believe will show them what is possible through hard work, it will inspire them greatly."

I put my hand to my chest and spoke. "Many years ago, I started my company to pay for a lifesaving operation for my son. I bought tea from you and sold it to my customers in America and paid for two operations. My son is going to become a strong adult one day, and it was you and your tea that helped to make it so."

As Gnana translated, I watched the eyes of the women and children. One of the women reached out and with big tears in her eyes nodded at me.

Gnana said, "We save each other by serving one another, Zeena. Thank you for this. These words mean the world to us, to them. You show us what is possible."

Gnana led me into the offices and the kids scattered onto the lawn to play cricket. I was poured a cup of black tea and offered warm milk and sugar. I sat on the couch and the group of women in peach saris stood in a half circle before me, smiling and observing me as I sipped the tea. Gnana sat in a chair next to me. "Zeeena, selling our tea in the USA, you have made us so very

happy, so grateful to you," he said. "You are making a big difference for our people here by supporting our vision."

My eyes welled up with tears again and I said, "I have been
selling it for three years. I ordered my first crate from your importer and I still have the crate in my office. It's been my motivation to get here, my beacon."

"Ohhh, very good, Zeeena, this makes us very happy." Gnana
nodded and the nine women smiled at him then looked back at
me. He said, "These are the tea worker representation body. They
bring the concerns and needs of the tea workers here to us so that
we can address each item and make things as good as possible
for them. They vote on where the fair-trade moneys will go each
quarter, and they have done a superb job serving the needs of the
workers in the entire estate."

Gnana explained the state of the garden when he and the new
owners arrived nearly seventeen years prior. They had held meetings with the workers, but the workers were not accustomed to
talking to management and at first wouldn't make eye contact
or answer their questions beyond a polite yes or no. Finally, the
workers felt safe enough to speak, and when Gnana again asked
what they most needed, they asked for access to toilets.

"The most basic needs for their dignity were not provided," he
said, looking sadly into his teacup.

Gnana and the new owners, headed by a gentleman named
Zaki Alif, visited the workers in their homes and found starva-
tion, anemic mothers caring for up to seven children, no running
water, and the men—depressed by having little or no work—were
abusing alcohol, which led to domestic violence. There was no
way for the mothers to get themselves or their children to the
hospital, as it was miles away and impossible to reach by foot.

"I was fired from my last management position for taking a mother and her sick baby to the hospital in my truck," he said, and shook his head. "They said that the workers could figure it out themselves. But children were dying. I watched the owners of these estates taking their dogs to the veterinarian, but when a worker or child was sick, they were to 'figure it out.' I vowed to create an estate where there was no separation between manager and worker, where we care equally for all people and living things."

Had I been born a tea worker, I might not have been able to get Sage to a hospital.

As if he knew what was going through my mind, Gnana said, "It is part of our long-term dream to create a place of health and happiness for all. Manager and worker are equal. The children must always be cherished. We are teaching them love, not fear. If the children are laughing, we know the tea will be good."

As he said this, we could hear the kids chasing the ball outside, talking excitedly and laughing. I became acutely aware of the peaceful energy of Gnana. It felt like he was a holy man, this garden his sacred temple.

Neesa said, "Zeena, we have been praying for your son." Her voice was quiet.

"Yes," I said. "He is doing so well, he would love it here so much. I'll bring him back as soon as I am able. He's mischievous, has red hair, loves sweets. "

Gnana said, "Zeena, Neesa's mother and father are both tea workers here, they are proud that Neesa helps me run the estate now." He smiled, and Neesa looked embarrassed. He added, "She was the first graduate of our computer-learning center, and she can use a computer, she's so much smarter than me!" He laughed heartily and all of the women laughed.

"Anyway," Neesa said, "you have inspired us, Zeena."

The first woman read from a thin piece of paper, "There are twenty-five hundred people living in the estate."

Neesa motioned another woman, who read, "The worker body represents all workers and is a voting democracy. We have voted a president to bring our voices together. She is a worker in the fields named Ranjani."

Ranjani herself then spoke, "We have five schools for young children and many more crèches to care for the babies. We have no chemical exposure. I came here from another estate to be healthy and have clean water for my children to drink."

Several schoolteachers spoke about their curriculum. The women completed their presentations, and each kissed me on both cheeks before leaving.

I said, "I'll share your story, I'll buy more tea. I'll bring school supplies next time."

After tea, Gnana and Neesa led me to the biodynamic composting and planning area of the estate, where they explained their growing methods for the tea.

"We believe that the tea plant is only one piece of the whole. We believe the roots, soil, farmers, tea workers, birds, insects, flowers, air, trees, sun, moon, stars, and planets all create a whole, and so planting, harvesting, feeding the soil, and nurturing the wildlife will lead to a better cup of tea.

"Nothing is separate, including you."

Neesa added, "Over here is where we grow the herbs that are used as a natural homeopathic tincture, our version of fertilizer." She led me to a row of herbs: chamomile, yarrow, valerian, dandelion, and horsetail. She said, "We make a tea from these and then use it to water the roots of the plants. Each herb has minerals that strengthen the tea's immune system."

Gnana said, "We also use ground-up crystals in the soil, energetically wonderful and full of silica to make the plant strong."

The next few days during my visit, I got to know the workers and Gnana better. I spent time with the children in their schools and visited worker families in their homes. This estate bordered another estate, owned by a different company. It was profoundly different looking. The plants were in rows, but not as full or bushy. The housing was in a line, the roofs made from sticks and pieces of metal flashing. Gnana stood next to me and waved to the workers. He said, "Zeena, we can convert more land. It's driven by demand. If we can create more demand for our tea, then we can buy other gardens and make them like this one."

On my last night, as I fell into the bed at the small guesthouse, I felt whole. The work I had to do to sell more tea in order to help spread the word about Gnana and the Idulgashinna business model would be enormous, but now I knew it was the truest, most vital effort. Where I had used his teas in some of my blends, I now wanted to change the formulas to use his tea as the base of all of them. My mission was aligned with his. I saw behind my calling and knew that I had not picked tea—it had picked me. That night, I wrote in my journal, *God is everywhere.*

When I returned home to the tea company, my tribe was waiting. Sage ran in first and everyone hugged him. I showed everyone the pictures and told them what our new mission had to include—increasing demand for organic, fair-trade tea. Everyone agreed we would do it and reworked the mission statement to say, "We provide health and happiness to consumers while alleviating poverty for tea workers worldwide." A wise consultant had once said to me, "With a mission to serve, you cannot fail."

Afterward, I walked into my office and saw a big pile of phone messages on my desk. Tristine, my assistant, followed me in and said, "I have some big news, Zhena. Safeway is interested in distributing the tea nationwide. They want you to go up to their headquarters. And a very nice man called who wants you to present to him and his team at Kroger."

My heart raced. I couldn't believe it.

"Wait, here's one more, Zhena. Have you heard of a place called Wegmans? I looked them up online and they are voted the best place to work in the US. A man called from there as well and said they'd like to talk to you about bringing the tea east into their stores."

I felt for my chair and sat down. I put my head in my hands so that I wouldn't burst into tears in front of her. I could hear Gnana's voice in my head: "Zeena, remember, those who can see the invisible can do the impossible."

Over the course of the next year, our volumes soared.

Answering the Call

Mantra of the Cup: I answer the call,
and experience wholeness.

You are an integral and precious part of all humanity. Your very existence was carefully orchestrated by Creation. Your soul has a crucial purpose and your job is to answer that purpose's call when it comes.

Emotions and yearnings are the language of your soul. They communicate to your mind from the deep code written within your heart.

What started with a yearning to meet the women in the tea fields led me to heal and integrate the many disparate pieces of my soul into one me. Meditation at the Golden Temple healed my residual fear from Sage's operations. Meeting the Queen of the Gypsies allowed me to confirm the ancient roots of my identity. Meeting the women in the tea fields allowed me to clarify and hone my mission.

I had felt a little sorry for myself until I'd met these women. Then I took nothing for granted. My fears that I wouldn't be able to increase demand were dissolved by the invisible interconnected energy of the sacred mission that I felt Gnana and I had spiritually joined forces to create. He taught me that kindness is its own reward and business can ultimately be a tool for healing ourselves and others. Business's calling should be to elevate others, not degrade or use them. Over the years of working with him, he would help me see that God's woodshop carves more than cups—it builds houses, schools, community centers, and bridges over which humanity can connect and flourish.

A selfless Gandhi in his love for his people, Gnana taught me that cultivating love in all things is possible if we are willing to respond to the invisible calls that pull at our hearts. Some calls are stronger than others, some lead somewhere, and some just lead to the next call. Acknowledging and heeding the call is the quest of your soul to grow; the outcome is not necessarily the point.

What is calling to you now? What call disappears only to return and linger? It doesn't have to make sense, because it won't necessarily do so until you answer. My call to the Golden Temple led to healing my fears and reconnecting with my legacy. My call to meet the tea workers led to my company finding its greater mission and to a massive leap in sales—from a small number of stores to mainstream grocery aisles across the nation. The call, the yearning, is not what it seems—it's a clue to what your soul's purpose on earth is. Are you ready to answer?

Exercise: Answering Your Call

This exercise will help you uncover and clarify a call you are being asked to answer. In your journal, finish the following statements:

1. I have a secret yearning to _____.
2. I have had this yearning for _____.
3. To answer this call, I first need to _____.
4. To continue to answer, I will then _____.
5. I will answer the call by _____ (date, time).

Many calls will come to you throughout your life. While not all of them lead to your destiny in full, each one leads you closer to it. Each helps you build trust within yourself in understanding your own powerful purpose that only you can fulfill.

> In order to carry a positive action, we must develop here a positive vision.
>
> —THE DALAI LAMA

11

Cultivate Curiosity

A Cup of Curious Combinations

*Curiosity will conquer fear,
even more than bravery will.*

—JAMES STEPHENS, *Irish novelist and poet*

*We keep moving forward, opening new doors, and doing
new things, because we're curious and curiosity keeps
leading us down new paths.*

—WALT DISNEY

Inspiration: Coconut Chai is a blend of sumptuously ripened coconut, thick and balmy Galle Valley black tea, sweet cinnamon, the bold heat of Burmese ginger, mellow nutmeg, prized imperial cardamom, piquant red peppercorns, and tongue-tingling clove. A godsend of innocence and spice, the blend was born of a healthy dose of curiosity.

This combination of sensual coconut and cinnamon essential oil dances atop a mid note of luxurious black tea. Close your eyes to taste the Sri Lankan rains and mysterious mists rising from tea leaves as day breaks. Gathered from all over Asia, each ingredient moves in its own direction, only to come together on the palate like the single beat of a drum. Sharp, spicy tinges are calmed and toned by mellow, oily vanilla beans, sun-dried on a southern Indian coastline. This blend brings out the global wanderer in us, adding comfort to the unknown road ahead.

The idea for Coconut Chai came to me on the streets of Colombo. The morning of my departure back to the States, I stood at a chai stall on a busy street, sipping some much needed comfort from a proud chai wallah's cup. I complimented him on the perfect balance of his blend and he beamed back at me. I was hours from heading home to Sage, and I had butterflies. Traditional milky chai at a street stall was a perfect send-off.

My first trip to Sri Lanka had been an intense whirl of emotions, awakenings, and transformation. I now had a moment to absorb them. All of the eye-opening revelations settled into my heart as I tasted the chai. Without really focusing, I gazed up at the swaying coconut trees, reveling in the steam and the sugar-cream flavor. After my third cup, a euphoria came over me. Drunk on chai, my eyes settled on the heavy coconuts resting and ripening in the trees above us, and I had a flash of insight. Where some see through beer goggles, I had chai goggles.

I thought, "I wonder what *this* chai would taste like with *that* coconut?"

After I returned home, I held on to the coconut chai inspiration long enough to blend it up in my kitchen. When I tasted the first cup after it had "formed" and the essential oils had soaked in, it surprised my palate, widened my eyes, and sent a warm message of perfection down to my stomach and all the way through my body to my fingertips. The chai reminded me of the selfless service I had witnessed at the Golden Temple. The soft spices filled my chest with warm wonder, the way Queen Sherma had stirred my soul. The bold flavor of the black tea took me right back to the heart of the Bio-Tea Project, where the children's laughter soothed the worries of the world. This was a kind of alchemical magic that came along only once in a great while. I took note, but then life kept happening.

I was really focused on business, business, business. Keeping it together for my son, employees, and the tea workers, I strived to control outcomes. My ability to take risks lessened, whereas it used to be my modus operandi.

My avid curiosity had always served me well. Leaving California to attend Cottey, a small midwestern women's college, taught me about the power of sisterhood; taking off to study herbs in Peru when I was twenty taught me to honor indigenous people and plants. Making that first trip to India and Sri Lanka showed me the power of vocation and a mission. But even though I had started my own business, my youth and lack of formal education felt like liabilities. To compensate for not having an MBA, I obsessed about learning business tactics. I read every business book I could get my hands on. I took online business classes while Sage slept and then strode into the office the next morning with new lingo and a sense of shaky bravado. I was determined that no one would be able to see that, most of the time, I didn't quite know what I was doing.

Still, it was clear from the books and courses that there was a difference between dreamers and visionaries. Dreamers don't necessarily engage with the rest of the world to achieve their dreams, but visionaries articulate their vision, act on it, and engage others in order to make it become reality. I strove to be a visionary and started to leave my dreamer at the front door of the company every morning. I plastered a veneer of leadership and worked my hardest always to be the one with the answers and never the questions.

As spring arrived, we were heading back into the slow season. Hot tea has much less appeal in hundred-degree weather, and we needed to trim costs to prepare for lower revenue. Since I had returned from the tea fields, we had added two more staff, which made us a tribe of eight people out to save the world. To keep everyone employed through summer, and to keep the fair-trade money flowing back to the workers, we had to comb the budget to cut any fat or dead weight.

At our weekly tribal gathering, I placed color-coded spreadsheets before each staffer. They sipped tea as I ran through the update, starting with the high points: sales were slow but growing year over year; we'd been featured in *Good Housekeeping*; and the remarkable spring harvest I had visited in Sri Lanka was on the boat, heading our way.

"Now, with the slow season approaching," I said, "we need to save up some cash reserves. And that means cutting underperformers. Honey Anise Chai, Honeysuckle green, and Lavender Fennel are all on the chopping block."

Everyone in the room nodded.

I went on, "Being 'hand blenders' doesn't mean we have to blend every single tea by hand anymore. If we can get to critical mass on some of these blends, then we can buy a real tea-blending machine!"

My assistant tea blender pumped a fist in the air. "YESSSSSS! It takes way too much time to stop everything and blend one single pound of a random tea. We need a machine!"

I waited a few beats for him to finish speaking. He was normally shy, and it was a good sign that he had such a strong opinion; he loved building cars, so I figured the idea of a new blending machine would be like a toy for him. And it would mean we were in the "big time" with the ability to blend a larger amount in a single hour than we could currently do in a whole day. The meeting was going well.

I looked back at my list and said, "And Coconut Chai is a bomb. Not the bomb I'd hoped it would be, but a bomb of next-to-nothing sales. So it gets cut, too." It had been months since I had blended Coconut Chai, but it was still at the bottom of the list.

The nodding stopped. Janine, my normally mellow and almost shy accounting manager, bolted upright in her chair and yelled, "You can't do that!"

"I know, I know," I replied. "I'm disappointed too, but—"

Jacqui, my office manager, or "girl Friday . . . through Monday," as I called her, said, "No, seriously, Z, you don't understand. We can't get enough of it. We fight over it. There's never enough to go around."

"Well, you guys have more adventurous palates than our customers, I guess." I looked down at the list and shook my head.

"But it's the best tea we've got," Janine said. "It's undeniable."

I felt the heated emotions rising from everyone in the room and realized I had to be the leader. "Look at the spreadsheet, you guys. How many cafés are ordering Coconut Chai?"

Jacqui ran her finger down the column and her face fell. "One," she said.

I stood as tall as I could, which is not very tall, and said definitively, "One café. We can't afford to ignore the numbers over a soft spot. It doesn't sell. I'm bummed, but it's got to go the way of the rest of the slower flavors, to the Land of the Lost and Dead Teas." I tried to be funny, but no one laughed. I said, "Okay, it's a wrap. Busy day. Thanks for your time."

I left them still sitting there and went back to my office, where I looked at the numbers again to be sure I hadn't missed something. Nope. Coconut Chai really was a dud.

There was a light knock and Janine poked her head in my office.

"I was just thinking," she said. "Why would orders be so small when it's so good?"

"We can't sit around and scratch our heads about that. That's why we have the numbers. They make these hard decisions easy, no?"

Her forehead crinkled. "But, don't you think—"

"I figured you'd be with me on this," I said. "I mean, we can't protect every underperformer. We're working too close to the bone. Fair trade, organic, kosher. We have so many expenses, we can't afford to make teas one pound at a time anymore. We're getting a little too big to stop shipping real orders, drop everything, and blend one pound of Coconut Chai."

Next Jacqui pushed into the doorway, "Besides Cameron, the almighty warehouse master, we all think you're making a mistake." Sarcasm was a strong suit of hers.

Mark, the web guy, poked his face between theirs, pushing the three of them into the office from the narrow doorway.

"Totally," Mark said. "Something's off. I've never tasted a better tea. I mean, I *dream* about it."

Janine rolled her eyes at him. "I'll say. He hoards a stash in his file drawer. Don't try to deny it."

"Come on, Zhena," Jacqui pleaded. "Aren't you even curious as to why it's failing so badly?"

I was, I realized. I really was. But I was so keen to have the answers that I'd become afraid of the questions. And now . . . well, if I was honest, I was just worried about being wrong in front of the tribe. My pride was getting bigger and my ego along with it. I was ready to shut down the subject and shut the door to my office, but that memory of being in India, the magic of each experience, and the palate-pleasing synergy flooded back to me. I took a deep breath.

When the rest of the staff crowded into my tiny office, I yielded, dialing the Coffee Cat Café in Santa Barbara, the one customer for Coconut Chai. I put the manager on speaker.

"Jenn?" I said. "Hey, it's Zhena from Gypsy Tea, and I have a question for you. We have to cut some flavors that aren't selling and Coconut Chai is one of them. You're the only café that buys it, so I thought I would—"

Her voice blared through the little speaker, popping with static. "Oh, my God! NO! That's our best seller! People drive miles to get a cup!"

"Really?" I said. "But it's only selling a tiny bit overall, actually just to you and my staff, apparently."

"Not my problem. If you cut that blend, I'll give our customers your address in Ojai to come and picket!"

I never would have thought that this one tea blend, out of all the things the café manager had to think about in a day, would have shown up on her radar.

"I admit," she said, "it took me a long time to try it, because it just sounded strange. I mean . . . who would put coconut in chai? But, if you cut it," she added, "there will be mass heartbreak all around."

The normally mellow Janine actually jumped up and down. "I knew it! It's not the flavor, it's the way we're *not* selling it!"

Mark ran toward his desk, saying, "I'm going to design a Coconut Chai page for the website!"

The tribe smiled at me with a joyful I-told-you-so! look on their faces, and it was settled.

Within the year, Coconut Chai became a blockbuster by our standards. It was the first flavor to get picked up nationally by the largest and most prestigious health food chain, and it was even promoted by Dr. Oz in *O: The Oprah Magazine*. It single-handedly put our little company on the map for many amazing new customers, and it would ride the coconut oil/coconut water craze into kitchens across America.

Cultivate Your Curiosity, Thrive in Possibility

Mantra of the Cup: I cultivate my curiosity.
I thrive in possibility and wonder.

Curious people are happier. As children we're full of natural curiosity, but as we grow up we're told that "curiosity killed the cat" and we start to see how it puts us at risk of potential failure. We stop leaping and dreaming and begin to play it safe. We form routines, and they become habit. Yet when we're attached to always knowing, we risk never growing. When stress, responsibility, or pressure is added to the mix, we are often tempted to control outcomes by knowing all the answers. In our rush to take care of business and check things off our list, we might leave some of the most valuable gems behind.

How do you cultivate your curiosity? To have a "beginner's mind" and learn as you go can be frightening, or at least frustrating. No business book or online course I came across gave instructions on how to be curious and vulnerable. Where I had once thought a leader had to know all the answers to be a success, I've now concluded it's the opposite. I've had to discipline myself to be innocently curious rather than importantly grown up, which leads to novel experiences and unlikely discoveries—like putting coconuts in chai or getting to travel the world in a teacup.

My friend Kira Ryder, a yoga instructor here in Ojai, is a wise and beautiful teacher. One day we met outside the bank and started one of our hellos that turn into hour-long discussions on love, livelihood, and longing. I asked Kira how she stays so present while holding space for the yoga students, and she said, "I stay curious. My mantra is, 'I wonder what's going to happen next!' I say it every day, because our lives are so much better and bigger than our minds can often comprehend. If we leave it open for the universe to provide the answers, we don't limit the options with our tiny human point of view."

Since this conversation, I say this almost daily: "I wonder what's going to happen next!?" It's invigorating to be open to the unknown, and I believe Kira nailed a universal truth: Our wonder can compel us to stay open to the gifts the universe is just waiting to bestow on us.

The exercise that follows gives you some of the ways you can redevelop and practice your natural state of curiosity.

Exercise: One Week of Wonder

For the next week, cultivate your curiosity by being open to the possible in all ways. Every day, take a different route to work. Ask a stranger, family member, or colleague a question you never thought you could ask. Offer to buy a friend lunch and interview her about a quality you admire about her, maybe one that you'd like to learn yourself. Make a list on paper or in your journal of the one action you will take each day that you have been curious about trying. The more curiosity and wonder you have, the more unexpected jewels can drop into your palms.

1. Monday: Take a new route to work, school, or the store. Take note of every new detail you see along the way.

2. Tuesday: Ask a happily married couple what their secret to long-lasting love is.

3. Wednesday: Ask someone you admire in business or work what he or she does to keep sharp and focused.

4. Thursday: Ask someone with a lot of money (or more than you) how he or she views wealth and how this perception might help you grow yours.

5. Friday: Ask a friend what she most likes about you and tell her what you most like about her.

6. Saturday: Ask a family member the hardest lesson he or she learned and what it taught him or her about life.

7. Sunday: Whether you are at church or a farmers' market, a beach or a park, ask someone what most inspires him or her.

8. Make a list of all you learned; as you notice your life expanding through curiosity, you may even discover that
   opportunities for prosperity, more love, and deeper spiritual awareness have been waiting for your notice. They'll
   bloom through your attention.

The great affair, the love affair with life, is to live as variously
as possible, to groom one's curiosity like a high-spirited
thoroughbred, climb aboard, and gallop over the thick, sun-
struck hills every day. Where there is no risk, the emotional
terrain is flat and unyielding, and, despite all its dimensions,
valleys, pinnacles, and detours, life will seem to have none of
its magnificent geography, only a length. It began in mystery,
and it will end in mystery, but what a savage and beautiful
country lies in between.

—DIANE ACKERMAN, *A Natural History of the Senses*

12

See the Forest for the Teas

A Cup of Perspective

We don't see things as they are,
we see them as we are.

—ANAÏS NIN

Inspiration: Caramel Chai brews ruby-red and feels like a hug when sipped. A reassuring blend of South African Rooibos with brown sugar creaminess, a generous dose of warming cinnamon, enough cloves to make you super kissable, a sprinkle of nutmeg to help calm your nerves, and cozy ginger to heat up your chest and body as you sip, it could be called "take it down a notch" tea. I use it as a reset button for my soul to regain a healthy distance from the day's labors.

I also use this recipe as a base for other teas—Christmas, Hazelnut, and Vanilla Chai. Just a tiny drop of a different organic flavor extract transforms this blend into new, succulent experiences. As in life, when something is good, it can pivot quickly to be repurposed, serving us a dose of perspective in the process.

As a mom-trepreneur, I was too busy to think about anything but the tea company and Sage. My life was a series of meetings, sales calls, trade shows, production checks, tea tastings, and learning how to manage a growing office tribe. This routine was broken up only by my son's frequent checkups and tests at the hospital. We would come back spent from UCLA Medical Center, yet we would head straight to the tea company, turn on *SpongeBob* in the pup tent I had set up for Sage, who was now four, work until he fell asleep, and then take him back to our little guesthouse. There I would get under the futon covers and stare at spreadsheets until I passed out—only to be woken before the alarm by worry, which would get us back to the office before the tribe arrived, so I could get a few things done before making calls.

Growing sales meant growing stress. The more the company grew, the more I felt the pressure on me mount. I found myself striving to ensure the poetry of tea was not drowned out by the business of it, but as we got bigger, that was harder to do. Although tea itself still held magic in the leaves, the business was a daily grind. I couldn't have predicted that our idealistic attempts at saving a small part of the world through tea entailed so much paperwork. Details of pallet configurations, trucking schedules, and trade show checklists permeated my dreams. My big vision necessitated endless tiny details, and holding them in my head left little space for much else.

The more we sold, the more opportunities there were for us to make mistakes. For instance, I was told by a grocery store on the East Coast that, when competitive companies wanted your shelf space, they could tell state-appointed weights-and-measures auditors that your product was missing servings so that the auditors would go to the store and measure your products. If the weight was off by even a fraction of a gram, the fines were upward of $15,000—per unit! Egads! Our packing was all done by hand, and human error with handmade products was an unfortunate yet inevitable part of the process. But if one light tin had ended up in New Jersey in the hands of a competitor out for the shelf space, we could have been put out of business in a matter of minutes. I became the world's most caffeinated micromanager at this point, scrutinizing every case of tea for inconsistencies. I couldn't control the competition, but I figured I could control each minute detail within our four walls. It was this or we'd meet our peril.

In one market, an aggressive company bought all of our tea off every store shelf at full retail, and then restickered the shelves with their price tags and simply took the space. A whole region and a couple years' worth of effort were gone in a week, done, finito. Years of work and investment were at risk if we took our eyes off the ball. I went from starry-eyed fair trader to warrior protectress in a matter of months. This new business reality jarred me. It held no reverence for the tea workers. It never considered the power of our mission. It threatened to make who we were in our hearts invisible. We had to compete like hard-ass businesspeople. I was knee-deep in trying to integrate this realization when we received our biggest order to date. It was for Christmas displays—a special two-hundred-display order with forty-eight tins in each—at a chain store in New Jersey. While the number at the bottom of the purchase order made me momentarily consider doing a backflip, when I looked more closely, I realized that it was *nine thousand six hundred* chances of being off by a gram. I grabbed the purchase order from the fax machine before the tribe could see it and pondered the massive task of packing that much tea perfectly.

I was explaining all of this to my main investor when she invited me to dinner.

"You need to meet my financial adviser," she said. "She's a total genius rock star in the investing world. She manages money for clients with five million dollars to invest, but she started with nothing, she grew her business and made herself from *scratch*."

"I'm too busy," I said. "And I don't have a babysitter," I added for good measure.

I also did not have $5 million and I wondered what I would talk about with a woman of such means. What would I even *wear*? Just hearing of her success made me feel embarrassed by my perceived lack of it. I had been blown away by an order that would net us $5,000—I couldn't fathom what it took to add so many zeros to that.

"My daughter will babysit. You're coming," she commanded.

My investor and I were going to the prestigious Ojai Valley Inn, a five-star celebrity and golfer hangout and a mecca for spa lovers and locavore foodies. I had dreamed of getting my tea in the inn but up until this point had felt too intimidated to ask. When we pulled up for dinner there, I shuddered. What if they wanted me to pay the bill? What if they expected me to buy wine? I checked my bank balance on my BlackBerry: $47.32. I could cover an appetizer and a glass of wine if we went "triple-Dutch."

I'd put on a really nice sweater I'd foraged from a clearance rack and my good pair of clogs. My investor and I walked arm in arm through the inn's gardens of lavender, roses, and rosemary until we got to the elegantly twinkle-lit outdoor restaurant overlooking the several hundred rolling acres of perfectly manicured, jade-green golf course. I felt my jaw relax for the first time in weeks. It was just so *nice* here. I felt a million miles from my warehouse, although it was only a few blocks away.

My investor's financial adviser—we'll call her Fae, for Financial Adviser Extraordinaire—jumped up from her seat, hugged my investor, and then beamed and hugged me.

"Oh, I have heard so much about you!" she said. "Sit, sit! I have a nice bottle of champagne on the way!" She patted the chair next to her.

I followed along as Fae caught my investor up on her many businesses and travel schedule. Then they both turned to me.

"So, tell me how it's going at the tea company," Fae said.

"Well, I think it's good. I mean, we're growing," I stammered. "People seem to like the product." I worked hard to find exciting news to tell her, but all I could see were my half-done to-do lists piled on my desk, along with that big PO that needed confirmation within twenty-four hours.

"I just love the product! I'm telling all my friends to buy it and how it serves such a good cause for the tea workers and, of course, our lovely friend here." Fae patted my investor's hand.

"Now tell me," she pressed, "I hear you've been getting some big sales these days."

"Yes, actually, we sold our holiday teas to the Vitamin Shoppe just a few hours ago. It's our biggest sale ever." I took a sip of the champagne, savoring it as the bubbles tickled my nose.

"How does that feel for you?" she asked and leaned toward me.

Feel? I didn't know how to answer that. "Um, well . . . I mean, it's a lot of responsibility. The tins have to be printed extra carefully because they're for the holidays and people will be buying them as gifts. And we've got to get them shipped by the twenty-first of this month or they'll be delivered late and who wants Christmas chai after Christmas? It's like selling a Christmas tree in January—impossible! Every little detail has to be perfect or—"

Fae interrupted. "Zhena, tell me, what's the first thing you do when you get a big sale?"

"I *panic!*" Oops, there it was, I'd said it. That wasn't the answer a successful financial adviser would be looking for. Then laughing it off, I added, "because there's so much that goes into it. I always thought tea would be easy, but there are so many tiny details, it's really hard to make it just right. I had heard that the biggest marketing budget wins, but I hadn't thought competitors could beat out our ideals."

Fae put down her glass and closed her hands in praying position. "Zhena, becoming a target for competition is an inevitable measure of a business's success—it forces you to up your game. Notice it happening, shore up the weakness it's exposing, and then quickly move on. Don't let competition paralyze you."

I was nervous, not wanting to show any weakness in front of my investor and her own adviser. Fae had the answers and I had more questions. I asked, "So how would *you* deal with competition?"

"When it comes to competition with a lot more money, there's only one thing you can do: Do what they *won't* do—not what they *can't* do. They can do anything with a big budget, but it sounds like they *won't* convert to 100 percent fair trade, because it's too expensive. They *won't* get their women-owned business certificate, because they're mostly men. They *won't* use organic tea, because there's just not enough of it." She smiled before adding, "And they *won't*, under any circumstances, take up palm reading and belly dancing in grocery aisles to promote their products. There's a lot of land for you to own, my friend."

We sat in silence for a few beats. I remembered some instances where powerful advice like this had landed in my life and reinvigorated my vision. Once, I had even shared a cup of tea with my hero—Dame Anita Roddick, founder of the Body Shop, who complimented the quality of Gypsy Love while giving me tough love of her own about my packaging. "This looks like it belongs in *Teen Magazine*, not in an upscale retailer! Your mission is bona fide, but your packaging is amateur!" It hurt, but when I followed her advice, we won design awards.

Another time, while I was serving tea in the Patagonia headquarters, founder Yvon Chouinard passed through the cafeteria and advised me to hire for passion and loyalty over the perfect résumé. "Hire people no one else will give a chance to, see their best, and they'll be their best for you."

Every piece of advice had come at a pivotal moment; it was unconventional and compelling; it motivated me to keep on. Little pearls like these helped me rediscover the unusual gifts of entrepreneurship—and of fulfilling a mission bigger than I was. And now I was receiving more wisdom.

I grew eager to honor Fae's advice and get on with accepting that order and face all of those details. Dinner amid all of this new insight seemed like an indulgence of precious time. "Thank you, Fae. I'm going to head back and get started on this big order. If I have it set up for the tribe in the morning, we can get on it."

To my surprise, she started to laugh. "Oh, my God," she said. "You can't see the forest for the *teas!*"

Fae looked at me as I sat in stunned silence, caught her breath, and continued. "Dreading success *repels* it, girl! Celebrating success *invites* it. Zhena, give yourself a moment to live in the joy of that big sale, or the universe will simply stop sending them your way."

My investor nodded and seemed relieved that Fae had said it so she didn't have to.

"Darling," Fae said, "when we begin to grow into our potential, we are often the last to know it because we can be our own harshest critics. Work hard, yes. But enjoy the benefits of that hard work. Look at where you are, enjoy a nice meal and some fresh ideas. Celebrate this moment without trying to control the next one. Zhena, I work with so many successful people, and you know what they all have in common?"

"What?" I asked and leaned closer.

"Perspective," she said as she smiled and held up her glass.

My investor raised hers and waited for me to follow suit.

I slowly raised mine, and as we clinked we made eye contact and said, "Perspective."

I had been taught that hard work was its own reward. Nobody had ever mentioned *anything* about celebrating. On Fae's advice, I began consciously to practice celebrating success instead of automatically defaulting to panic. My sense of perspective slowly dawned. Weights and measures became less daunting. Competitors looked slightly less big and scary when I focused on successes rather than them. I could see the positive things that resulted from my hard work, rather than just waiting for the other shoe to drop. By lightening up, I became more adaptable and had faster response times.

Celebrating isn't self-indulgent. It actually adds spaciousness to the hard work it takes to manifest a dream. It can lift our daily reality a little higher, making us "lighter on our feet" so that, when the other shoe does drops, we won't be under it—we'll be too busy dancing.

See the Forest for the Teas

Mantra of the Cup: I celebrate the gifts of the universe.

Panicking perpetuates scarcity. Scarcity guarantees a lack of options. With a supertight budget, it's hard to feel like you can celebrate a tiny win, but by celebrating it, you lift yourself up from scarcity and into a higher realm of possibility. Being discouraged is part of the territory you cross when following a dream, but by focusing your attention on what is working and good, you invite more good. Celebrating doesn't have to mean spending. I often advise my coaching clients to take a walk on the beach or spend an extra hour with a child in celebration of a win. Celebrating says to the universe, "Bring it, I'm ready!"

What do you do when you have a success? Worry? Dread the moment you might lose that success? Or do you spend some time savoring it?

So many brilliant ideas don't stand the test of time because the originator loses perspective. We succumb to that feeling of disenchantment that accompanies bringing a dream into reality. On the mountaintop, we can hear our call, but then as we carry that call down into the world, we encounter naysayers, distractions, burgeoning details, and resistances. We have to be strong enough to bring our call into reality anyway while doing our best to enjoy the process of creation. The only way to power past resistances is to keep perspective. Perspective is the cure for the challenges we face when we are breaking through our current reality in order to build a new, better one.

Perspective is always hand-delivered to me by my friend and meditation teacher, Jagat Joti. Let's call him the purveyor of the world's finest and funniest perspective tools. He was my first consultant at the tea company more than a decade ago, and he still has a knack for unexpectedly texting or calling at just the right moment, day or night, to deliver some perspective via a joke, anecdote, or story from his guru, Yogi Bhajan. When he first taught me to meditate years ago, he called me a "blender without a top." It was tough to hear, because he was right. I was all over the map, and my efforts weren't getting results. Meditation helped me focus, which changed my results from meh to wow—while giving me some serious peace of mind. He also gave me the gift of the invisible "times-zero gun" for shooting "bad guys," which helped when I was dating and getting dumped. I multiply anything by zero and it just, well, vanishes from existence. Same with fears, insecurities, and doubts. When I was having debilitating insecurities in a family relationship, he told me to pick a piece of lint off my clothes every time the person made caustic comments. I practically unraveled a sweater one Christmas, but it worked, and I laughed—a lot—as I "picked" the negativity off me.

You gain perspective as you learn to reward yourself for life's little graces. I'm not talking about going on a bender in Vegas every time you see progress. Just enjoy a moment, a breath, a cup of your favorite tea, or some music in acknowledgment of your effort. Absorb the goodness sent your way for a job well done. This allows you to rise above the minutiae every once in a while to see the big picture—a picture is usually brighter than you expected.

Exercise: See and Celebrate a Success

Make a list of things you accomplished in the last twenty-four hours. Start with waking up, and then keep writing. Write for at least five minutes or until your hand is exhausted. Look for actions and behaviors—"I smiled at the bus driver"—or a kind gesture—"I made coffee for my friend." Everything you did in the last twenty-four-hour period is important. After you have written all you can remember, take a look at your list and hone in on any step you took to realize your dream. Then notice the actions you took for love, out of generosity, with others in mind. These are the miracles *you* made. These make you a miracle worker. Celebrate these things!

Did you carry out any kind acts for yourself? This is also a miracle, which you can celebrate simply by recognizing it. So much of our lives go unnoticed. Acknowledgment is a celebration in itself. So many moments pass without our noticing their existence. How can you start to notice and celebrate little acts of kindheartedness that you do? The hard work and big milestones are important to notice, but so is the hug or smile. These little luxuries affirm the magic of living. Notice them, appreciate them, and enjoy them and they will make you more thoughtful, mindful, and exceptional. This is perspective.

> There are only two ways to live your life.
> One is as though nothing is a miracle.
> The other is as though everything is a miracle.
> —ALBERT EINSTEIN

13

Without Hot Water, the Leaves Impart Little

A Cup of Character

Change your opinions, keep your principles;
change your leaves, keep intact your roots.

—VICTOR HUGO

Inspiration: Biodynamic Darjeeling green tea. "The agony of the leaves" is the term used to describe the unfurling of the tea leaf when steeping. The character and complexity of the tea are held in reserve until it is exposed to boiling water. Only then does tea infuse the water with its elegant palette of pithy floral high notes, soft herbaceous mid notes, and a base note of transformation and transmutation. Tea can take a tough day and convert it to a journey of your soul.

Everything worth anything must be steeped perfectly. A tea is considered forgiving when you can abuse it with the wrong temperature of water, bad timing, and oversteeping and it still tastes good. An unforgiving tea can steep for only a short time and still risks growing bitter, its tannins pronounced and drying to the tongue. One of the most prized teas in the world is Darjeeling, and it's unforgiving. When steeped incorrectly, it becomes bitter. Some say alcohol brings out one's true nature, but this tea brought out mine.

At the height of the housing bubble, people were financing houses to double their worth. Money was easy; scarcity seemed a thing of the past. I remember someone joking that he used to live "paycheck to paycheck," but now he was living "re-fi to re-fi." Upscale, organic products were seeing a surge in sales and price was no longer an issue. The term *ultrapremium* was becoming more commonplace as luxury brands hit the mainstream. I noticed people were drinking better wine, biodynamic wine, craft beers, and loose-leaf teas in fancy silk tea bags.

With this exciting cycle in the economy, I decided to split my line into collections the way fashion houses do. I wanted to have "everyday drinker" teas and ultrapremium teas for special occasions and causes. When I heard that the largest natural retailer was looking for more biodynamic products, I realized that I had a chance to bring the beauty of biodynamic farming to people on a broad scale. I saw ultrapremium and ultra-organic converge and become my new line.

"We believe biodynamics are the next big thing for our market," the buyer said. "Make me a biodynamic tea, and we'll launch it nationally and develop your brand for exclusive sale in our stores."

I said, "I'm your girl!" I knew biodynamics because Gnana's garden was the first to get certified, and he had taught me the power of this farming method to heal the soil and produce profoundly better teas. There, they fertilize the soil with organically grown herbs like yarrow and chamomile, and add ground quartz crystals to boost the tea leaves' levels of silica, a nutrient with cancer-fighting attributes. Instead of pesticides, Gnana lures pests away from the tea bushes by a perimeter of colorful flowers—companion planting turns out to be both beautiful and practical. The soil was so alive and well cared for that the plants could withstand any disease; they were so vital that they practically glowed. Just remembering them motivated me to do everything in my power to translate their beauty into a tin of tea. I was poised to seize this opportunity because I was already using his and others' biodynamic teas as the base for all my blends.

I called it "Beyond Organic." Instead of our regular hemp paper sachets, I sourced biodegradable silk made from non-GMO corn. Instead of labeled tins, I printed them with elegant, enticing new artwork. And I formulated five new teas that were from solely biodynamic sources, which would allow me to call them biodynamic certified—a designation reserved for only the most rigorous standards worldwide. Gnana had very clearly related to me that biodynamic farming was the answer to healing the environment, and I leapt at being a bigger part of the solution. I loved the idea of melding the ultimate environmental mission with a sensual, haute-couture line of ultrapremium teas. Ultrapremium and superorganics dovetailed perfectly with the demand of a huge chain, so this was my chance to go supernova in all the right ways.

Our volumes were high enough to develop signature flavors and to contract out to farmers for raw ingredients. This was a vastly different experience from when I was first going organic. This time I had scale, a platform, and a famous retailer's commitment to launch it with me. A flavor house in Europe signed on; they too were impassioned by the challenge. I developed five very *Gypsy Tea* flavor combinations that also met the stringent guidelines in order to be certified: blueberry-vanilla, mango-ginger, kiwi-peach, caramelized pear, and Black Forest berry. While the uncommon flavors would attract adventurous tea drinkers looking for an expansive new culinary experience, the biodynamic aspect would attract wine aficionados, tea lovers, passionate environmentalists, and purists alike.

It was exhilarating having a customer this big awaiting the product. I had the chance of a lifetime to explore the outer realms of creativity and sustainability in one fell swoop. With a guaranteed purchase order, which was a rare and fortunate luxury, I could develop a line that would make the news! Organic and fair trade were great, but launching a biodynamic line of innovative flavors in a big national play was a powerful way to lead the industry, expand our brand, *and* impact the world in a positive way. If consumers could buy caviar eye cream, I figured, they would leap at the chance to go Beyond Organic with us! The sun, the moon, the stars, and our tea! It was bound to succeed, because not only was our heart in the right place, the conditions and consumer climate for sustainable luxury were ripe.

It also gave me an extraordinary chance to translate the magic of my deeply affecting experience at Gnana's to the rest of the world. It was an opportunity to escape the minutiae of business for the poetic essence of what I knew to be sacred in tea. I delved 110 percent into the process. With the help of a high-powered brand consultant, a savvy graphic designer, we designed new packaging that was understated and upscale, not our typical, flamboyant, brightly hued, hand-drawn look. We figured the product was complex enough; we wanted the packaging to tell a concise story.

I knew my buyers and customers would want to know how any one product could take so much work from seed to soil to cup, since that extra care would show up in a higher price. While organic is chemical-free, the tea may not be as fortified as a biodynamic source. We launched an education campaign explaining this "superorganic" process, touting the higher polyphenols and antioxidants made available to the plants through highly nourished soil. I also tried to impart the mystical experience of visiting the biodynamic tea farms: the pristine beauty, the birds flocking in the sky, the bees buzzing as they collected pollen from the nearby flowers, and the superior health of the tea workers that all combined to create a rhythmic "energy" that could be tasted. It was love made evident with soil and grower, flower and field, tea maker and consumer, where all elements and souls harmonized. The beauty and effort it took to grow tea in this method were so life affirming that I was sure every single person on the planet would be moved to share in the miracle that it is. Because it was true for me, I thought others would share my epiphany about biodynamic farming.

"This product line is going to make us a big success," I told the tribe, "bigger than I could have imagined! The market is catching up to the mission! We are leading the way for the entire industry! We are category-creators!"

The product rolled onto the shelves in a big way, and the new tins looked like heaven—with sky, soil, roots, and, above the sumptuous fruit images, a new brand name: Beyond Organic.

With the promise of widespread, national distribution of the line, we'd bought a year or more's worth of raw materials; because there are so few biodynamic tea gardens in the world, we needed to ensure we didn't run out of the precious ingredients. We committed to an entire year's harvest of a garden in Darjeeling and blended it with Gnana's treasured, choice green tea, added the flavor extracts, essential oils, vanilla beans, ginger chunks, mango, and berries, blended them, and then put them in the corn silk fabric in individual servings and gingerly hand filled each tin. It took tremendous care. The flavorings were delicate and the silky fabric tore easily since it was biodegradable and not nylon. We did everything with the highest standards and the results were spectacular. Flavor, appearance, scent, sight, and mission met at their apex in this line of teas. We were all so proud.

The first month was one of sparkling perfection as orders flowed like a paper waterfall through the fax machine. We were written up in the press for starting a new category in tea—one of the highest sustainability standards. For all of the hard work that had gone into every aspect of the company for so many years, this launch felt effortless. *Brandweek* magazine called the line "Eye candy on the shelf." One reviewer wrote, "The greenest green tea I've tasted is also the tastiest!"

As sales piled up, the tribe got so excited that they came early and left late. We wrote the daily sales tally on a big chart on the wall. Just looking at it made us happy. I put bells on everyone's desk, and each time they got a sale, they hit the bell and we all clapped and cheered. I took them out for drinks to celebrate. I envisioned giving out generous year-end bonuses for big holiday smiles. I visualized my bank account balance growing finally, validating the enormous love I had in my heart over tea and our mission. Our superorganic tea was big! And I was superwoman at my super company in a super lucrative time in the world! Yay, me!

Then one day the stock market fell. Orders dried up. Like a drop of water on a hot blacktop, there was no trace of a sale to be found. The retailer who'd developed us for the superpremium market started getting negative press for being too premium. The tea stopped selling and they stopped ordering. There was even a backlash against organics because of their cost. The demo reps reported back that those customers who sampled it balked at the $12 price tag for only fifteen cups. They said shoppers were avoiding anything that wasn't bread, butter, milk, and the basic food groups. We went from our biggest sales month ever to the lowest.

I hid in my office, curled up in my chair, and read the financial news as it hit the Internet, feeling paralyzed. Bank after bank collapsed and the politicians battled over a bailout. People were in over their heads and underwater on their houses. I couldn't expect anyone to care about my esoteric dream of healthy soil in a land nine thousand miles away on the other side of the earth. I racked my brain for a way to revive sales and make biodynamics relevant in this new market. But no matter how long I stared at the spreadsheets, the numbers weren't changing, and neither was the news. The product sat on shelves, one retailer referred to it as a "museum piece." Meaning it didn't move. Yet we had packed huge amounts, thousands of cases. All of our working capital was tied up in the inventory.

After a week of sitting in my office, agonizing over what to do, I hauled myself up and headed outside. As I trudged up my favorite hiking trail, my mind feverishly played out drastic scenarios. Furlough the tribe or, worse, lay them off; lose the business; end up living in my car. Other single moms worked for me, depended on me. I blinked away the distressing images of them packing up their desks.

At the lookout point, high above the town, I surveyed my rural community, wondering how they were handling the financial meltdown. I contemplated the new vineyard that had replaced a citrus grove, wondering if the change had been a result of inclination or economic pressures. In the last recession, a premium wine company had made news by changing their label from a high-end look to a dust bowl image à la *Grapes of Wrath*. They had called the vintage Recession Red and lowered the price from $25 to $5. I hadn't even been old enough to drink it, but it had made an impression on me. It was a *smart* compromise.

I couldn't relabel the Beyond Organic line of teas, since the tins were already printed with the elegant new artwork, but I could sell my highest of high-end product at any price I could get for it and at least make payroll. A blast of chilly fear washed through me. I had made it to the top shelf, and it was a long, frightening fall to a discount store clearance rack. In grocery terms, it was a "reclamation expense" on the profit-and-loss statement that was so big it could destroy the years of passionate work we had put into the company. If store buyers and luxury customers saw this lofty, ultra-premium tea in clearance houses, would my company become a joke? An obvious goner? Would they doubt the value of biodynamics?

It had taken Gnana twenty-five years to build up his biodynamic farm, and it had taken three months for me to fail at my own dedicated line of biodynamics in the Western marketplace.

I considered that my business might end up a casualty of my ambition. Maybe it was time to harden my heart, put some salaries on the chopping block, and redouble my marketing effort. Protect the brand or pay the tribe?

"Oh, for heaven's sake, Zhena," I thought as I stood on top of the mountain. "It wasn't that long ago that you were hunting down the discount-store twofer in order to eat.

"Actually," I corrected myself, "you couldn't even afford those stores when you were 'dating to eat' those years. So, rich, poor, or in the middle—you are still you. Premium or pushcart, your tea is a loving extension of you, and people need the healing and comfort more than ever, *wherever* they may get it."

In my frenzy to go big I had gotten brittle, hardening up against the embarrassment of being seen as having jumped the gun, backpedaling on my ideals, or throwing a type of cheap and desperate yard sale on my most precious product, one that I had touted as the ultimate prestige product in a new category of tea. It took some hot water to remind me who I really was: a girl who grew up shopping in discount stores. The recession took me back to my roots when my waitress mom and US Forest Service firefighter dad had to stretch dollars to put food on the table for me, my brothers, and all our neighborhood friends. The image of the roots on the newly designed packaging now had a greater meaning, it took me back where I belonged, to the roots of America and my upbringing.

I took a deep breath, and as I let it out, I allowed the image of that high-end, high-design future float away over the valley stretched out below me. If discount stores were the ones growing in the deepest of recessions, we would go there. The word *exclusive* had started to mean "out of business" to me. No matter what our mission was, if our company wasn't around after the recession, there would be no mission.

Selling to discount retailers kept us going through those tough times. They literally saved our business. We didn't make any money from the teas, and our brand took a beating with the exclusive-minded folks who wanted something hard to get. But we had opened people's eyes to the value and quality of biodynamic farming methods and we had found a new set of consumers that would become our most vocal and loyal customers when the economy started to perk back up.

Without Hot Water, the Leaves Impart Little

Mantra of the Cup: My character shines in lean times.

Hot water can allow for the "unfurling" of our best, highest selves. I thought I'd wanted to be exclusive—a fancy pants of tea, if you will. But through this failure, I found that my character really valued being accessible and approachable—and ultimately that saved my company from extinction. The failure of the Beyond Organic line got me closer to my deeper nature, showed me who my true friends were, and made me more open to my path. The mission survived, but the hot water of my situation purified me of that ego need to be seen as exclusive or part of the über-premium brands.

When you are immersed in difficulty, self-protection is your first instinct. But if you can allow hardship to soften rather than paralyze you, you can find out what you're really made of. Failures are inevitable; they are our gatekeepers to success. If we fail at one market, we can find our true market. Our resilience in these "hot-water moments" teaches us crucial lessons of where we can grow from here.

My dear friend Brenda represented my tea with a natural products brokerage in the Rocky Mountain region. A top sales producer, she always made me feel like my tea had the care of the best. One day, Brenda realized she couldn't do it anymore. Fourteen-hour days, hardly any time with her three kids, exhausted from a failing marriage, she filed for divorce, quit her job, and filed for a business license all in one week. She had hit her boiling point and knew her whole life had to change. The hot water showed her that she valued being self-reliant and she unfurled and made a brave move. She started over with nothing, yet went about building what is now a leading firm representing sixty product lines, covering ten states, with employees spanning the Rocky Mountains and Southwest. Brenda's values of honesty, independence, humor, and empowerment are now embedded in each of her employees as well as her kids. She could have become Brenda soup in all the hot water she was in, but she looked at her values, saw where they weren't aligned with her life, and tapped the motivation to align herself with them.

Even Brenda fails a lot. She says, "Hot water comes and goes throughout life. It doesn't just go away, but don't let it intimidate you. Sometimes all you can do is grieve, reflect, breathe, get your emotions under control, and then respond. Figure out what you can do in that moment and do it."

Getting into hot water has a purifying effect on our nature. It shows us who we can be and who we might not want to be any longer. Hot water sent me right back to my roots and showed me my market, and it allowed me to develop the customer loyalty I craved and needed to grow my business, and my character.

Exercise: Steep Your Greatness

Reflect on a tough moment, disappointment, or failure in your life and watch for any residual sadness or grief that is still within you. Now shift your attention to consider how you've handled tough situations in the past. Write down which traits you relied on.

1. When the going gets tough, I rely on _____ to get through.

2. Hardship and challenge show me _____ about myself.

3. I admire _____ about my character.

4. When in hot water, others can count on me to be _____.

Now think of something in your life that you know needs to change . . . but hasn't. Examine it, write it down. It can be a relationship that drains you, a financial situation, a hurt or worry, anything. Now take your answer from #4 and see how it can help you in this unresolved situation. See yourself successfully adjusting the challenge by using this trait to transcend it.

You are amazing.

> You cannot dream yourself into a character; you must hammer and forge yourself one.
>
> —JAMES ANTHONY FROUDE

14

See (for) Yourself

A Cup of Self-Validation

What we achieve inwardly will change outer reality.

—PLUTARCH

Inspiration: Bergamot that goes into Earl Greater Grey. Bergamot is often used as an antidepressant in aromatherapy and its tea brightens tough days with gray skies. Bergamot holds a glow that helps us see the possibility in any situation. It inevitably comes to our aid when we need to see the best in ourselves, as we sip its sunshine essence and its invigorating, bright ruby-toned infusion. My formulation of this uplifting blend is a rich, bright, liquored steep of Ceylon black tea as the base note to a particularly heady, aromatic, and intoxicating organic cold-pressed oil of bergamot citrus fruit that comes from a group of small artisanal farmers in Sicily.

Every year end, I couldn't wait to call my dad and tell him the tea company's numbers. The calls would go something like this:

Me, in a trying-to-be-cool-but-obviously-excited voice: "Dad, guess what? We sold twenty-five thousand dollars' worth of tea this year!"

Dad, in his standard monotone voice: "That's nice, Zhena."

Then he would comment on the rainfall that year. We'd talk about what kind of fire season we were likely to have, and I would hang up the phone and feel depressed for a week.

A retired firefighter who still grades fire roads on national forest land in the off-season, my dad is of Ukrainian descent and was born shortly after my grandparents arrived in sunny California. You'd never guess his mother was my passionate Grandma Maria who shaped my own wild spirit. My dad didn't speak English until second grade. His home life was so different from that of his classmates. At my grandparents' home, it was still the Ukraine— the food, the belief system, the strange superstitions—while at school and out in the world, it was 1950s America with big beautiful cars, bobby socks, ponytails, and outgoing girls. He kept to himself and, as my mom explains it, was nearly invisible until she decided at age fifteen that she was going to marry him.

Dad remained unimpressed as I built my company. Every year we worked hard to get our sales to grow by leaps and bounds, and every year I hoped the number would be big enough to crack my dad's reserve with a smile of astonished pride.

When we broke $100,000, I knew *this* would be the phone call to shake loose some big praise.

"Dad! Dad!" I said. "Are you sitting down? Because I have huge news! HUGE!"

This was more money than I'd ever seen, more than anyone in the family had ever made, more than I'd dared to dream of making.

"That's nice, Zhena," he said, and then added, "But that's how much you *sold*. How much did you *make*?"

Well, if you looked at it that way, I *was* still barely able to pay rent, so $100,000 wasn't that impressive after all.

"So . . . you got some rain out there, huh?" he asked.

Then the following year, it happened. I flew through the glass ceiling, did a few laps around the moon, and when I came down to earth, I landed right on top of the million-dollar sales mark. It was a tremendous sum, a massive accomplishment. One of my biggest dreams was to see the number of woman-owned businesses in the million-dollar earning zone grow dramatically in my lifetime. Now I'd done my bit to boost that number and, I hoped, bushwhacked a path for other women. I was ecstatic. I couldn't contain myself. It was happy dances and hugs all over the warehouse, and then I skipped to my office and called Dad.

"DAD, GUESS WHAT!?!?" I screamed. "WE EARNED A MILLION DOLLARS IN REVENUE! CAN YOU BELIEVE IT? WE'RE IN THE BIG LEAGUES NOW!!!!"

"That's nice, Zhena," he droned. And then there was silence.

I felt for my chair and sat down.

"Did you know that less than two percent of woman-owned businesses ever make a million dollars in revenue?" My voice came out angry. I was mad.

"That so? Hmm." He was silent for a couple beats, and then asked, "Did your landlord do the fire clearance yet? You know, you're in the line of fire if we have a big season."

My heart went from bursting to deflating. My dad's inability to understand the odds that I had beaten nearly broke my heart.

I hung up and looked at the seven-digit number on the screen. It no longer seemed so big or great. I calculated the cups of tea it took to get there: twenty-two million cups of tea! *A lot of tea!* And every single cup counted to me, but not to the most important man in my life, my dad.

I kept doodling numbers on a piece of paper and felt waves of sadness that no woman should ever feel when accomplishing her dream.

The thing I'd been living for—my dad's approval—was never coming. I vowed to stop calling. It was just too painful to keep reaching for something he couldn't give me. But not calling didn't help the hurt. A local businessman who mentored me told me what I needed to do.

"Nothing outside of you can make the inside feel better," he said. "Self-validating people do not look to others for their worth, because they know who they are without external confirmation."

I wanted to be one of *those* people. I loved the term *self-validating* and kept repeating it over and over in my head for days. I wanted to cultivate an internal compass for success. There were twenty-two million cups of our tea in people's kitchens all over America. Why couldn't I see the value in *that*?

I started seeing a therapist and worked my way through the stack of self-help books my mentor sent me home with. I worked at self-sufficiency and practiced patting my own back. It wasn't easy, but I began to accept that the appreciation I thought I needed from my dad had been inside of me all along. I understood it intellectually, but my heart still ached for his approval.

I was making great progress, when the company achieved another big milestone. *Real Simple*, a favorite magazine of mine with a ton of market sway, wrote up our Earl Greater Grey. After tasting two hundred teas, they named it "Best Earl Grey in the Nation"! It was HUGE news, validation that was substantial and real. As if that wasn't exciting enough, the acknowledgment resulted in a blizzard of sales. I was seized with the urge to call and crow about it to my dad.

But instead, my self-validator told me to hang tight. So I marched myself over to my sitting cushion and meditated. Then, despite the urging of my hand hovering over the phone, I went on a loooong hike. Once I was back home, I wrote in my journal, played with Sage, and read him every Shel Silverstein poem in every Shel Silverstein book in the little apartment. When he fell asleep, I sat on the floor and did visualization exercises. Still the stubborn urge remained to call my dad. I lit candles on my altar. Then I rearranged my altar, which led to rearranging my furniture and straightening the few pictures on the walls, anything to keep me from picking up that phone. And little by little, a glow formed around the achievement while I stayed quiet about it. We were the smallest of the companies represented in the "best of." It delighted me to think we were the "little tea company that *could*."

The next day, with my office door closed, I opened the tin of Earl Greater Grey and breathed in the sweet, uplifting aroma. To my surprise, it seemed to fill the part of me that felt so empty. The scent filled me with deep joy all by itself.

It's hard not to get addicted to validation. I mean, a group of people who didn't know me had tasted my tea all the way in New York City and reported back—to the nation—that it was the best. It was so gratifying and so satisfying, yet it went against the idea of being self-validating. As I held the tin of Earl Greater Grey in one hand and *Real Simple* in the other, I took another deep breath and absorbed the excitement that was trying to drive me back to the empty well at the other end of the phone line. I sat through the waves of desire that flooded me and did not call my dad.

Sometime later, I needed to go to the Sri Lankan tea fields for the harvest. When I called to see if my travel dates would work for my mom to watch Sage, my dad answered.

"Hey, Dad. Is Mom there?"

"She's not home, but I'll have her call you." His monotone didn't budge a note when I told him the news of my big journey, but I was okay.

"So how are you?" he asked.

"Oh, good," I said. "Just working a lot."

"That's good. Working hard is how we get anywhere in this life."

I made small talk. "Yeah, we couldn't get the pallets of tea on the trucks anymore with the hand truck, so we had to buy a fork-lift last week."

"You *did*?!" I heard an upward inflection in his voice for the first time in my life. "A forklift? Wow, that's *amazing*! Electric or gas? What kind of cage does it have? What's the turn radius? Pneumatic or cushion? How many pallet racks are you putting up?"

He was . . . excited.

"*Now?!*" I screamed inside my head. "Now you're impressed? A million dollars puts you to sleep, but a *forklift* gets you going?"

Then I pictured his face, animated and smiling under the John Deere cap he always wore, and I had to laugh. "Of course," I thought. "Heavy equipment—that's something a firefighter and road grader can get excited about." I indulged myself in a long and detailed discussion about forklifts with my dad.

See for *Your* Self

Mantra of the Cup: I sip from an endless well of love and appreciation; each breath I take validates me.

Do you have a place in your life that you are consistently looking for others to validate in order for it to seem more real? Sometimes it's hard to know when we are doing it, but bringing awareness to the times we grasp for approval can heal the need to rely on outside influence to fuel our motivation. Once I stopped chasing after the elusive pat on the back, I was able to turn a feeling of loss and emptiness into appreciation for who my dad actually was, rather that perpetually trying to get him to be somebody else for me. Our whole relationship healed and my achievements became more real and resonant within me. I could then see him and validate *him*. At my urging, he started his own road-grading business, with his own heavy equipment. Now we talk about strategies, P&Ls, setting fees, and revenue. Turns out, he needed to be seen just as badly as I did. I was so busy trying to get his validation that I didn't see he really needed mine. Two seekers don't always make a right, but by being present to another human's needs we are able to be present for our own.

Is there a place in your life where you are holding back love from yourself or waiting for someone else to provide you with it? Once you realize you are seeking validation from someone who is currently unable to give it, that awareness helps you to become your own source of nourishment. Notice where you are seeking approval and give it to yourself. Once you begin to notice and value the place where you're seeking it externally, the world around you follows suit. Sounds easy in theory, but is this as easy in practice? It is if you have an example to live by.

My example comes from my friends Gay and Katie Hendricks, who are well-known relationship mentors. Every time I see them, they take notice of something specific in me and compliment me on it and acknowledge it in a meaningful way. At first, it made me feel uncomfortable. "Yikes, they're really looking at me!" But then I learned from them and began to realize if I could just emulate their practice a tiny bit, I could grow appreciation for my employees, my son, and all those in my life by a simple method they model.

Gay and Katie will notice something, and say things like, "Zhena, I wanted to tell you that I really appreciate the enthusiasm you bring to everything you do," or "You know what I notice about you that I really like?" They look me in the eye, hands on my shoulders or touching my arm, and give me all of their attention while delivering their "I see you" statements. Being around them is so uplifting and invigorating because I know through their words and acts that they value me. It takes them all of thirty seconds, yet the result is profound. When I've practiced this myself, I marvel at the way people bloom in the light of appreciative words.

I recently met Anne Mahlum, founder of Back on My Feet, a for-purpose nonprofit that helps people experiencing homelessness to join running teams that build confidence and purpose. She has everyone in her running groups say one thing they love about themselves. She says this is a crucial way to gain self-confidence—but we often hesitate or have a hard time naming one thing. Name one thing you love about yourself. Was that easy, hard?

All we really want is to belong and be appreciated in life, and Gay and Katie have become my model for this art of seeing and validating others. It didn't come naturally to me—I'm my father's daughter, after all—but I love seeing its positive effects in my relationships. Here's a tool to grow this goodness for yourself.

Exercise: I See You

Today, look for traits, habits, and characteristics in yourself that you like. It might be that you automatically smile at strangers or you crack yourself up. Maybe it's the way you make your tea or coffee just right. Whatever it is, write it down. Do you make pretty flower arrangements, have a uniquely organized underwear drawer, or always remember to water the plants? The small things that you are good at matter, so list them. Dig deep for subtle things, under the surface, things you really LIKE about yourself. Use the words, "I appreciate . . . ," then add your trait. Once you have a list of five to ten things, review it.

Now, if you want to take this a step farther, to really cement the practice, create a list for your mate, a friend, your boss, a family member, or your kids. Pick out the subtle things you like about them and share it with them. The reverberation of that appreciation will deepen your relationships in profound ways.

> I've talked to nearly thirty thousand people on this show, and all thirty thousand had one thing in common: They all wanted validation . . . They want to know: "Do you see me? Do you hear me? Does what I say mean anything to you?"
>
> —OPRAH WINFREY

15

Allow Kindness In

A Cup of Kindness

*Too often we underestimate the power of a touch, a smile,
a kind word, a listening ear, an honest compliment, or the
smallest act of caring, all of which have the potential
to turn a life around.*

—LEO BUSCAGLIA

Inspiration: Ultimate Green with matcha is an uncommon flavor combination of lychee and apricot with white and green teas, pure powdered green tea matcha, and lemongrass. It's blended as a health serum with the addition of green tea extract for heightened immune function, anti-aging benefits, and calming nerves. L-Theanine, an amino acid found in high concentration in matcha, gives this tea the power to focus and soothe the mind's worry and negativity, and impart gratitude. It also holds within its fine powder the healing properties to restore a broken heart.

This blend was inspired by the wisdom of a UCLA surgeon and the kindness of a tea-serving stranger when Sage was having what we hoped would be his final operation—the one that would free him from the treadmill of pain and procedures he'd been on for all of his four years.

I had gone about building the business motivated by the need to protect Sage and to provide enough resources for his health care. The company's group health plan allowed Sage to be covered as an employee child member, which was a major milestone. I had worked with a fury, learning my lessons all for his benefit and safety. Before that final operation, each moment of each day had a shadow over it. I feared that his health might not improve, that I might not have the means to help him, or that the doctors would come out of his monthly tests with some irreversible bad news. I overcompensated for my fears with a frantic, hard-driving energy, which made me appear tough and intense on the outside.

I walked through life weighing everything's importance by how it affected my son's health. I tried to control Sage's environment, fed him foods that kidneys need to rebuild, and gave him every natural supplement I could find to bolster kidney health. The control was hard to turn off and on, and so I carried that persona with me everywhere. In addition to an army of medical specialists he saw, I consulted with every natural healer nearby, spiraling farther and farther into debt. Besides Gnana, only my family, Sage's dad, and the tribe knew of his illness, because I was scared to acknowledge it and embarrassed by my lack of resources for him. I also feared—irrationally, as many mothers with sick children do—that I had done something wrong when I was pregnant to cause him this suffering.

When the day came for Sage's final operation, in the waiting room of the operating room at UCLA, the kindly Dr. Churchill lifted Sage out of my arms, patted my shoulder, and smiled reassuringly.

"Now, you need to leave for four hours," he said. "I don't want you back any sooner than that."

"No, that's all right," I said. "I want to be here in case he needs me."

The previous surgery had hurt Sage's condition more than it had helped. I wanted my presence in the waiting room to protect against any such complications this time, so I put down my cup and grabbed a magazine. I wasn't going anywhere.

Dr. Churchill was patient but firm. "You have to understand that there's nothing you can do now but take care of yourself. Get out into the sun."

Sage reached for me and I started to cry.

Dr. Churchill did not relent. "Go. I mean it. You have to go, now. Your worrying won't help. See you in four hours." He looked at me sternly, and then walked away as Sage looked over his shoulder at me.

I pushed through the exit doors and stepped onto concrete that seemed to give under my feet. This surgery was the most important conclusion to four years of constant worry. I'd taken Sage to the hospital for blood tests every time he had a fever, watched and examined his facial expressions for signs of pain, and kept him out of water, which could contaminate his incision. He had always been safe and secure in my arms, or else playing in my line of vision.

I walked down the crowded sidewalks of Westwood and circled UCLA, praying, holding back tears, and willing the surgery to go well with every muscle in my body. When I finally looked up, I saw a sign that read GREEN TEA TERRACE and felt a little ripple of gratitude. A cup of tea; the idea felt like a lifeline. I pushed open the door to a matcha boutique teahouse with pale celadon-colored walls, simple décor, a wall of teapots, and a glass counter. The small, bright space was comforting. A smiling young man said, "Welcome. You look like you could use a cup of tea."

"Please, a very strong matcha," I said and dropped into a chair at a little table in the back corner. My insides were shaking. My jaw was clenched, my lips were pursed, and my heart was aching. I tried to scrape up some faith. I trusted Dr. Churchill. I envisioned him holding Sage. I pictured my son's skinny little body curled up in the doctor's long, all-encompassing arms.

The young tea purveyor gently placed a teacup in front of me. The bright green foamy matcha swirled clockwise as I looked into it. I tried to smile, but it felt like a grimace. I murmured thank you, head down, afraid to make eye contact in case it would break my concentration on Sage's perfect healthy outcome.

The jade liquor smelled vegetal and sweet, like freshly cut grass. When I sipped, the foamy, ceremonial-grade green tea coated my mouth, and as I swallowed, the hot green liquid calmed my raw nerves, focused my mind, and settled my swirling, worried thoughts.

The bottom of the cup appeared and, before I could ask, the young tea purveyor stood next to my table with another. He whisked the green elixir, and I watched the tea circle the way the rings of Saturn gather around their planet. Each sip swept another web of worry from my mind.

The young man reappeared at my side and put a third cup of matcha in front of me. I looked up to protest. I wasn't sure I had enough cash . . .

He put his hand on my shoulder and offered a knowing and comforting you-are-going-to-make-it smile.

"It's on the house," he said.

His kindness dissolved the tension that had been holding me together. To my horror, I started to cry. I grabbed a paper napkin and tried to hide behind it. "I'm so sorry! It's just that my son . . ."

"Shh, I know. A lot of moms come in here. We're a sort of haven for wayward, worried mothers. They come in with a dark cloud over their heads and leave a little more optimistic, a tiny bit less stressed. I dispense the medicine of matcha. It's all I know to do." He couldn't have been twenty.

"How did you get so wise?" I sniffed.

"Me? Wise? Hardly. But when I graduate from med school, I'll know how to help. I want to be a pediatric surgeon." He added, "I got a scholarship and work here for my living expenses. I never understood the power of tea until I got this job. Now I'm a huge believer. Tea really is medicine."

With the next sip, the truest thing I could know entered my thoughts: You are going to be able to face whatever is next.

Dr. Churchill was smiling when I walked into the pediatric ward. He took my hands. "It went beautifully."

I felt his encouraging words everywhere within me and I exhaled for the first time in almost four years.

Sage lay in the hospital bed, still unconscious. I sat next to him and looked at the tubes entering his little wrists, the catheter tubing coming from his tiny abdomen. I rested my head next to him and let myself cry. The hard outer shell cracked open. I stayed this way for an hour or so, just releasing the tears that I'd kept at bay for so long.

Then I heard a little whisper. "Mama, it's going to be okay. Mama, I promise."

Sage's bright green eyes were open and tinged with concern. I smiled helplessly at him.

If a wise surgeon hadn't thrown me onto the street with his tough love, I wouldn't have received the kindness of the young tea server that helped me pull myself together. I had never been so vulnerable and I had never felt so strong.

I pushed a red curl off of Sage's forehead. "Yes, it is. It really is."

In my blind determination to be strong for my son, I had almost become brittle and in danger of breaking. From now on, I would try to stay soft enough to receive the sometimes unsettling nourishment of kindness that is everywhere.

Accept Caring from Others

Mantra of the Cup: I allow others to fill my cup
with kindness.

Our culture applauds us for "soldiering up," for being "tough as nails," for being everything to everybody, and for never needing anything for ourselves. But when we allow worry to harden us, when we are afraid to be open and soft enough to receive comfort, we can eventually find ourselves at the end of our reserves. At this point, we're no good to those who need us.

Years ago, I had fallen in love with a guy who didn't love me back. In fact, he dumped me over the phone on the morning of the Fourth of July when Sage and I were planning to see the fireworks with him. I got someone to watch Sage and then spent the rest of the day crying in the bathtub while I called each and every friend and sobbed uncontrollably into the phone. I kept calling my friends back after they listened to the first rant, as I had more to cry out. Oh my God, I had been convinced he was The One! Eventually they stopped answering the phone. Then I got a text invite to a big party that night. I figured that since Sage was cared for, I would go, and in perfect scorned-woman-fashion I got dressed up, put on twelve layers of eyeliner to cover my swollen, football-shaped eyes, and went to the party to show the world that this guy couldn't get a good woman down.

At the party, I practically hid in the shadows while nursing a glass of wine. A group of women were dancing together without men. They were beautiful, strong, dressed to kill, and having SO MUCH FUN. I felt so empty, and they seemed so full! During a band break, the tallest one made her way over to me and said, "Hey, little Goddess, what are you doing all the way over here? Want to dance with us?" Her beaming grin unraveled me again and I said, "I got dumped today and I feel like I'll never find love!" She grabbed me in a bear hug and said, "Oh, little one, it all gets easier, just close your eyes and pretend you're forty, it'll all be okay!" This was my introduction to Sunne Justice and her group of friends she lovingly referred to as the Goddesses of Ojai.

She urged me to visit her the next day. When I arrived at her beautiful home, the Goddesses were waiting for me. Sunne was adamant I have time in the sun with her Goddess necklace, and as she put it on me, the weight of rubies, emeralds, and sapphires around my neck rendered me speechless. I had never in my life seen such opulence, but Sunne said she invested in it the way others would buy bonds, and it was therapeutic—jewels heal a woman's heart, she said, forming us into higher-vibrational women—think Cleopatra, Princess Di, the stars in Harry Winston on the red carpet. I suppose this was from her time as a merchandise director at *Vogue*, and it couldn't have been more alien to this country bumpkin of a girl. The necklace belonged in a museum, but according to Sunne, it was a means to claim our royal femininity. It worked. I healed from the broken heart as Sunne and her circle of women took Sage and me under the span of their jewel-hued wings.

Through the years, Sunne taught me to allow others to fill my cup by modeling her own acts of mindful generosity. When I needed sales at the tea company, she gifted me with a fluffy pink robe and told me to make sales calls from home in it, which led to my first major sale with a huge chain (as Chief Pollinator of Burt's Bees, she knew about sales).

One Christmas, when I was struggling financially—as usual—Sunne invited me over to exchange gifts and tidings for the season. I had very little funds for gifts, and I always felt a bundle of nerves around the time of year, hoping no one would buy me anything so I wouldn't have to scramble to afford something back. I gave lots of tea to friends and family, but Sunne, ironically enough, doesn't drink tea. I went to the local New Age store and found a small sphere of labradorite for her altar. It looked like a tiny crystal ball. We sat in her living room, amid Romio Shrestha's celebrated Tanka paintings of Buddha (the originals, no less) and exchanged our gifts. She opened hers first and oohed and aahed over the little crystal like it was the most precious of gems, and she transformed it into one with her praise of it. Then it was my turn. I opened my gift and it was a Goddess necklace—a real one. Real gold and semiprecious stones and pearls with beautiful artisan gold handiwork. My jaw couldn't be found to even begin closing it. It was the first real gold jewelry I had ever owned.

I was so embarrassed over the small gift I had given her. She forced me to put the necklace on when I tried to give it back, for fear of never ever being able to repay her. Gifts like this just didn't happen in my life. Afterward, she put on her own necklace, and we danced around the house with glasses of organic chardonnay to the beats of Krishna Das. Every once in a while she would pick up her little crystal and dance with it, thanking me profusely. Laughing, dancing, beaming, sipping, thanking, and being. Somehow that night, Sunne taught me that money was a tool to lift up others rather than a thing to fear. My belief in a constant dogmatic and even-steven reciprocity at all times never allowed me to receive the way-out-of-proportion gifts the universe was attempting to give me. I always thought I had to return everything in the exact quantity as received—gifts, compliments, time. Sunne's generous gift healed a big part of my poverty mentality, which was blocking friendship and care.

Is your cup open and ready to receive, or do you have it turned over so nothing can be poured into it? We often dodge generous people or acts of kindness because we think we must repay them in full, or that the person giving may have an ulterior motive. But does she? Often, the person attempting to fill your cup with kindness is doing so from the heart. She needs no payment other than your sincere gratitude, because she is acting on behalf of God.

Exercise: Your Cup Runneth Over

Sit a minute and sip from your teacup. Remind yourself that strength pours into you from unexpected sources. Breathe in the steam and allow it to soften you for receiving. Breathe out and release the weight you've been carrying. Close your eyes and visualize others' kind acts toward you throughout your life: a hug, a gift, a warm embrace, a kind word, a touch when you needed it most. See each act in your mind and transfer it to your cup. Now open your eyes and sip from the cup, absorbing the kindness that has been given to you. Allow it to deeply nourish and remind you how others love to fill your cup with their affection for you.

We are cups, constantly and quietly being filled.
The trick is knowing how to tip ourselves over and
let the beautiful stuff out.

—RAY BRADBURY

16

Surrender to Your Promises

A Cup of Night-Blooming Jasmine Nectar

Love makes your soul crawl out from its hiding place.

—ZORA NEALE HURSTON

Inspiration: The vines of jasmine that intertwine with the high-grown *Camellia sinensis* plants perched on the ledges of the rain forest tea fields in Haputale, Sri Lanka, mimicking the perfect union of soul and body. A hand-tied white butterfly tea is scented with the ephemeral perfume of night-blooming jasmine blossoms. The little white flowers sprinkled into this tea burst in your mouth like a French kiss. When this rare tea is sipped at night, under a full moon, while planets glimmer up high, its spell ensures your love will stand the test of seven lifetimes. It can turn a guarded woman into a wildfire. One sip of this precious and rare potion opens a woman's heart and body like a sacred flower. One sip for a man, and he will sensually explore his lover's erogenous zones, as if her body is the universe, because he realizes it *is* the universe.

I was madly in love with a man named Gerard and I couldn't believe he loved me, too. He was so handsome, polite, responsible, successful, sexy, and even funny. He could be über-professional in a suit and tie and domestic and thoughtful at home, always jumping up after a meal to do the dishes. I didn't have time to mess around with men who weren't serious. I was a mom with a growing business, so I took Sage on our third date. We met at Paradise Cove beach in Malibu, and Sage allowed himself to be bribed with french fries, telling Gerard all my secrets—exposing my most flawed self.

At almost five years old, Sage had established to Gerard that he wouldn't allow another man to hurt his mama. On date four, under the stars at the Hollywood Bowl, Sage demanded to know if Gerard loved me.

"Yes," Gerard stated, matching Sage's sober tone.

Sage wanted proof. He pointed to an imposing security guard.

"If you love my mom, go kiss that big lady on the cheek."

Without hesitation, Gerard went over to the guard and explained his orders. Her severe expression evaporated and she sweetly held out her cheek for Gerard to peck.

Sage crossed his arms with an air of satisfaction. In his mind it was settled. In my mind the war of doubts was just beginning.

Here was a guy so good that he got up at 4 every morning to meditate. He never drank too much. He actually finished what he started, daily. A world traveler, he had visited castles in Transylvania and bat caves in Belize. He laughed like Amadeus, making my own cackle seem almost dainty. His class voted him most likely to be president.

He'd had a privileged upbringing in Orange County in a big house with a pool, while I grew up in a neighborhood where people sold crack and as small children we played in the streets with no shoes. I was messy, busy, and feral. In the Los Angeles area with its millions of beautiful women, he'd picked a short, single mom who toiled long hours for her small business and lived in a tiny guesthouse an hour and a half away in Ojai. I wanted love, but I'd learned since Sage was born that no guy was ever ready for the whole package. When they found out I wasn't going to back-burner my business, my kid, or my mission and make them the white-hot center of my world, they left. I'd been through this a few times and so I worked extra hard to scare Gerard off even though it would break my heart in half if he left. But he kept steady. He showed me over and over that no matter how much I pushed back, he would stay put. He joked he was the "Gypsy whisperer."

He proposed to me on Mother's Day in Big Sur, as we touched foreheads, sitting on a felled log over a creek. I said yes before the words were even out of his mouth. I cried and laughed, kissing my new fiancé's cheeks. We held hands, swung our feet, and I spent the next hour saying the beautiful word *fiancé* over and over again, feeling the word form deliciously in my mouth and fill the air around us like a sacred chant. In that word was also the idea of stability. Finally, a family of three.

As we headed back down the hill, I remembered a promise I had made several years before. I said, "Gerard, I promised Gnana Sekram, our tea estate manager in Sri Lanka, that one day I'd be married in his tea garden." I paused when I saw him frown a little, adding, "I have to keep my promise. I know you might want to get married here, with our families, and this is a lot to ask . . . but I promised."

He turned to look at me. "Zhena, you know I love to travel, but . . . we haven't even been engaged for an hour . . ."

"It's a place I can't easily explain, but it explains *me*," I pleaded.

"Babe"—he leaned down to look into my face—"it sounds like a *great* idea. No family, no headaches, no expectations, just a small little affair in a tea field with no fuss. Sounds perfect."

I was relieved, and I took this as a sign that he really did know what he was signing up for.

When I told Gnana the news, he gave his gentle rolling laugh. I could hear him smile through the phone as he said, "Zeeena, you have kept your promise, and now it's our turn to help you have a blessed married life." But as soon as we announced our wedding date and set up the travel to Sri Lanka, the universe seemed to protest. First, Gerard's jeweler lost a four-carat blue sapphire intended for his wedding ring while they were sitting in the car looking at it; it was never recovered. When the replacement arrived in the mail a few days later, it was cracked. So Gerard had no ring. In the taxi to the airport, the stone escaped from *my* ring. When I hugged Sage goodbye, my prized meditation necklace, which had been blessed by a monk for our safe travels, broke. All of the amethyst beads disappeared down the airport street drains. Then, we were not allowed to board the plane because my passport had fewer than six months left on it. We spent the next four days at the government building in L.A. trying to get a rush replacement. I sobbed the whole time. I felt it had all been too good to be true.

When we finally arrived in Sri Lanka, almost six days late for our own wedding, we discovered that the sari and jewelry I'd bought for the ceremony were all wrong. In his humble office, Gnana took one look, shook his head, and said, "Zeeeena, you are one with these people. We want you to wear exactly what one of them would wear at her *own* wedding."

He held my intricately embroidered sari to the light, and the glittering crystals looked rich and out of place. Even though I'd been proud of it moments before, it now looked ostentatious. I had completely forgotten humility in the sari shop in Colombo, when bride frenzy had taken over and I'd gotten more excited over each offering. As the sari seller pulled elaborate saris from the shelves, each was more lavish than the last. Finally, when the sari dealer went to the back room to get the "crème de la crème" for me to see, he'd brought the hand-embroidered gold Swarovski crystalline sari and I *had to have it.*

Now, in the humble tea office, doing the math in my head, I realized that the cost of the sari, while pretty low compared to an American wedding dress, was more than the annual income of a tea worker. I'd made a fair-trade faux pas. I also worried Gerard would think me insensitive.

Even more disorienting, Gerard and I had been prepared to have a small, quiet, nonimposing Buddhist wedding, but Gnana told us we would be having a Tamil Hindu ceremony, because that was the religion practiced by the workers. The ceremony would be held in the Lakshmi temple on the tea estate. The goddess Lakshmi cares for the poor and offers abundance and prosperity to those who call upon her. I was thrilled because I had paintings of Lakshmi all over the tea company and a big altar with offerings of milk, honey, and flowers for her in my office. She looked on peacefully as our tribe fought for shelf space and brand awareness in the Western world, and we attributed to her the daily miracles of our mission. She was our holy mascot, our goddess-in-residence.

When our wedding planner, Dayan, heard this, he shrieked, "You can't just switch religions like that!" But soon he realized it wasn't just our wedding.

Yet another complication occurred when the Hindu priest informed us that before he would marry us, he had to do our astrology charts in order to see if we were compatible. *Compatible?* Wasn't it too late for that? I didn't want the priest to look at our charts. The stars had been throwing tacks under our tires for weeks. What if he saw something we weren't ready for or, worse, what if he told us there was no way our union could work?

Sensing my distress, Gerard whispered in my ear, "I'll marry you no matter what he says."

After a day of much deliberation at the Hindu temple, the priest announced that Gerard and I were in fact compatible. But we had to change the day of the wedding in order for it to be auspicious. And the Tamil ceremony called for a wedding necklace—a Thali—not a ring.

Now I needed to have a wedding Thali made, find and fit a new sari, buy flowers for the bouquet, and rent a traditional Tamil Hindu jeweled wedding set. Gerard had to have a wedding ring made and now that we knew his Vedic astrological chart, we had to find the right stones that would bring about health, wealth, and success. Gnana would rearrange all of the workers' schedules to shift the wedding date.

"This is a lot of work," I whispered to Gerard. "I feel bad that we knew so little. Poor Gnana has to do all of this when we wanted it to be so simple for him."

"He has a spirit of total generosity, Zhena, and he obviously cares very deeply for you." Gerard squeezed my hand and I reflected on my relationship with Gnana.

My heart swelled with gratitude. I was his customer, but he had no obligation to organize our wedding. He could have granted my wish to have a tiny ceremony in a small corner of the tea field, but he cared about my relationship to the workers so much that he was making it their wedding, too. Successful business relationships are defined by financial gain, but Gnana's and my ROI was also defined by love. I'd kept a promise and now Gnana was rewarding it with the caring focus of his entire estate, bringing our wedding into the lives of all twenty-five hundred tea residents.

The local sari shop was very different from the one I'd visited in Colombo. Instead of bejeweled designer saris on model-like mannequins, it had thousands of brilliant bolts of color stacked up the walls like a rainbow library. We settled on a rich pink-and-gold satin sari. It cost twenty dollars. The one I had bought in Colombo had cost nearly a thousand.

As soon as we walked into the little red-velvet-walled jewelry shop, I saw the perfect wedding ring for Gerard with a yellow sapphire.

Gnana said, "Ahhh, yes, very good luck!"

"Oh, I really wanted a blue sapphire," Gerard said, "but we lost one and the other was cracked."

Gnana tilted his head. "Blue sapphire is the stone for hard lessons. Bad luck for a wedding ring with your astrology. Yellow sapphire is for wealth, prosperity, happiness, and joy. A much better choice for you."

"For your wedding Thali, Zeeena, I have chosen for you an *om* symbol, which will bring you much peace in your married life," Gnana said with authority, adding, "You cannot take this Thali off until you die . . . or your husband dies."

In the back workroom, three Tamil men sat on the polished

dirt floor making refined gold jewelry with small, blackened tools. An oil-wicked flame flickered in an old coffee can from the quick movements of their hands. Gnana explained what was needed to one of the craftsmen, who nodded and smiled. Hunched over the flame, he formed the gold loops of chain, sealing them with quick motions, then wiping the black from the gold to reveal its shimmering pattern. While Gerard and I watched, we said little vows about our love and life together, so that each link was infused with intention.

At Gnana's guidance, we generously tipped the jewelers for their beautiful work and Gnana went up front to negotiate for the jewelry. The chain, *om* pendant and wedding ring came to $500. So much gold, and it all cost less than the original wedding sari.

The morning of the ceremony, Gnana's assistant, my friend Neesa, put the tailored sari top on me; it was so tight that I could only pant to breathe. Once it was zippered and buttoned, it forced a roll of fat out from under it, which was on prominent display since the sari exposed my midriff.

"Oh, my, Neesa, how do we cover this?" I pointed to the roll of fat.

"A sign of beauty," she said, smiling.

"Not in my world." I didn't think I wanted Gerard to see my belly looking like a shar-pei puppy, "Can't we hide it?"

"Zeeena, it is truly considered attractive here. I am not lying, I promise." She patted my shoulder.

Neesa deftly folded the layers of the sari and pinned them to my skirt. Then she added the jeweled headdress, ear coverings, earrings, barrettes, armbands, nosepiece, bangles, short necklace, long necklace, and belt over the sari and pinned the long garlands of jasmine flowers to my hair so they would trail down my back.

Then I went into the garden to meet Gerard, who was wearing a simple cream-colored Indian suit and scarf with a long dark gray Indian-style vest. He looked understated and classy, while I felt like an explosion of paint and tinsel.

But he stared at me and said, "You are my goddess," and then gently kissed my cheek while I fought back happy tears.

In front of the temple, hundreds of people stood waiting for our arrival. The tea workers were beautiful in their best saris, and I hugged and kissed those I knew. Gnana led us to the temple as the factory workers beat drums and blew horns and the tea pluckers threw jasmine flowers in the air above us.

Handmade garlands of red, green, and yellow folded paper birds interspersed with garlands of betel leaves were strung like chandeliers overhead. From the raised wedding platform, I looked out at the sea of beaming faces. Each woman's dazzling special occasion bindi sparkled from the center of her forehead, making a glittering star field as they bowed, repeating, "Namaste, namaste."

One of the tea managers carried the red velvet box that held my Thali, my engagement ring, and Gerard's wedding ring. Every person in the temple touched the box and made a quick prayer over it. When we were handed the rings, we put them on each other's fingers, and then Gerard put the Thali around my neck, which shone in the light of the flames.

In accordance with tradition, the priest had Gerard vow that he would forever see every other woman as his mother or sister and only me as his lover. Then he asked me to vow to see every other man as my father or brother and only Gerard as my lover. Then Gerard draped a bright red sari over me, as instructed, and with this vowed to buy me beautiful dresses and adornments for the rest of his life.

The priest declared us married and told us that we were united for seven lifetimes. Gerard and I giggled at that.

"Thank God, I *like* you so much," I said.

We were led to the back of the temple, where a shimmering altar with a stone statue of the goddess Lakshmi stood, draped in a pink-and-gold satin robe with red and yellow carnation garlands hanging down to the candles flickering at her lotus feet like little flashes of sun. Incense danced in rhythmic wisps around her as she looked on with the half smile of the ephemeral.

"You have one whole minute to ask Lakshmi for anything you want," Gnana said. "Whatever you ask for now will come to you and be true."

I got on my knees before her and Gerard did the same. Given the opportunity to ask for anything I wanted my mind went blank. I pushed my forehead into the ground and whispered, "Think, think!"

What I thought was, "So many years of struggle . . . I want a house, a pool, a million dollars, a Mercedes, a trip to Paris, a month off, to never be sad or worried, and for Sage to live happily, forever."

I took a breath, inhaling into my pounding heart, hoping this would allow my soul to communicate with my head in order to get my request to the exalted goddess who waited, according to tradition, for my "ask."

Instead of my desire for expensive creature comforts, I whispered, "Dear Maha Lakshmi, please help me to be there for Sage and Gerard, please help me be there for these beautiful people who have done all of this for us. Please help me repay their generosity. Please help me love bigger and better than I know how to, please help me understand God's plan for my life. Please help me help Gnana in any and all ways possible . . . Please help me . . ."

In mid "please help me," I heard a melodic sound like wind chimes gently clinking in a slow breeze. No words came forth but the sound, the high-tuned jingling moved like a river through my eardrums. It carried my attention and I raised my hands, cupping them together in receiving pose. Eyes still closed, a small, bright light appeared and then grew bigger and bigger until a living, breathing Lakshmi stood before me on a pink lotus, the universe swirling in her eyes, her cloaks glinting and glowing the color of Venus. She smiled at me while I looked on, breathless. She said, "Open your fingers like rays." I obeyed, taking my tightly cupped hands and fanning my fingers open. She filled my hands with gold coins, and as they touched my palms they multiplied before falling from my fingers. The coins flew from my hands in infinite directions, spreading to each and every person in the temple, then out to the tea garden. She spoke, "As long as you give, I will give to you. You are here to *serve.*"

Just then, the priest announced our minute was up. The silence gave way to the beating of drums and blowing of horns, clapping, and laughter. I returned to the present moment, traveling back from another dimension—was that other dimension my heart? I rose shakily and exchanged glances with Gnana. He saw the surprise on my face. I wondered, "Did he see what just happened?" I put my hand to my heart and smiled. The joy of the divine had entered there.

I had a *destiny.* "You are here to serve." I repeated these sacred words in my mind, savoring each syllable like a fine wine.

For the first time in my life, outside of the times I spent caring for Sage, I understood that I wasn't at all who I thought myself to be. My life wasn't about *me*. It was to serve. Serve others, serve tea, serve spirit. Serve Sage, my husband, and these glorious souls. *Serve for serving's sake.* I remembered being so struck by the Sikhs' serving *dahl* outside of the Golden Temple that I wanted to learn how they could be so generous and gracious. My desire to emulate them was actually my purpose on earth.

We were brought to a small brass bucket, and Gnana explained that in the muddy water were a ring and a conch shell and that we were to plunge our hands into the water and retrieve whichever one we could. We would play the game three times. I felt my competitive streak kick in and grinned widely up at Gerard. I wanted the ring.

The first time, I easily grabbed the ring while Gerard willingly brought up the shell. The second time, he fought a little more for it and I still got the ring. The third time, he went after the ring, but it floated right into my hand. Gnana and the priest laughed and the crowd all laughed, too.

"You, Zeena, as a woman, are an incarnation of Lakshmi," Gnana said, grinning. "The one who gets the ring is the one who attracts the wealth into the family, while the one who gets the shell has the job of protecting the money."

The final phase of our ceremony required the parents or representatives of the parents of the bride and groom to give us their blessings. Gnana brought forward a Hindu elder, a monk, dressed all in white with three white stripes across his forehead.

Gnana introduced him. "Zeeena, Gerard, this is the high holy priest of Tamil Hindus of Sri Lanka." Gerard and I both got on our knees and touched his feet. We had no idea that the high priest of the island's Hindu faith had been with us throughout the ceremony.

"He will act as your father, Gerard. And I will act as yours," Gnana said, smiling at me. Then he added, "It is very auspicious for him to join us. He donated this land to us almost twenty-five years ago and hasn't returned to see what we have done with it until now, at your wedding. Very auspicious indeed. Oh, such a blessing for our people."

Gerard and I were both greatly humbled by this. I bowed again to him as the holy man placed vermillion on Gerard's forehead. Gnana and his wife did the same to me. In that moment, Gnana became the spiritual father of my marriage, just the way he had been to my business. The circle was complete. Gerard and I were married and had seven whole lifetimes to enjoy each other.

Outside, a long table held massive clay pots of steaming dal, rice, and vegetable biryani. The tea estate families waited patiently in line for us to serve the first plate of food.

We stood at the beginning of the serving station and the first child held his plate up to me. I spooned a big heap of vegetable biryani onto the plate.

Gnana quietly whispered into my ear, "Zeeena, be extra generous with them. There is plenty. This could be one of the biggest meals of their lives."

I looked down into the child's brown eyes, smiled, and piled as much food as would fit his plate.

While I was fretting at the airport over the loss of some beads, these tea workers were depending on me to be strong and help sell their tea to the Western market for the price it was worth. In this garden, the beacon of fair-trade gardens, there was still need. There was so much farther to go. "Please allow me to truly serve these people," I thought, imagining Lakshmi pouring coins into the serving bowls.

Gerard watched me closely, and I wondered if he was going to be able to handle my commitment to the tea company's mission. I would be in the tea fields and away from home.

Gnana said, "Go, now. Sit and enjoy yourselves. You have had a very successful, auspicious wedding, and I am sure you are tired."

"No way," Gerard said. "I want to keep doing this."

I looked up at my new husband with gratitude.

He smiled at me and said, "I get it now, baby. Why you work so hard. You've got me to rely on now."

And with that, I stopped nursing my doubts and insecurities about him. Gerard had married me with his eyes wide open, he *knew* me now. All of the things I could not explain were now in his spiritual DNA: the love, the children's laughter and big soulful eyes, the precious moments shared with these women who need a voice in the Western world, the beauty of the land, and the sacred bond with Gnana. He had experienced my highest good. The universe had been extra generous with me by giving me my son, the tea company, and the love of these remarkably generous people—I needed to receive it all fearlessly.

We served every person twice. The fluffy golden rice, buttery dal, fried vegetables, yogurt raita, and sweet chutney never ran out. We served some people thirds, and when finally all were sated, we made a plate for ourselves and sat.

Our arms were tired, we were tired, but we were beaming. The food was so spicy that my eyes poured tears, and the black, oily eyeliner that had threatened throughout the ceremony finally did run down my cheeks. I had to remove the clasp of hanging beads from my nose, since it was running steadily from the tears and hot chilies.

Neesa ran over to me with a disapproving look. Her creation was coming undone and while she wiped my eyes with a wet napkin, I grinned at her like a child: mascara streaking, nose running, mouth on fire, and heart totally, finally, wide open.

Surrender to Your Promises

Mantra of the Cup: By making and keeping promises,
the delight of the Divine is mine.

Resistance is the gatekeeper of our divine purpose. The promises we are driven to keep, despite the resistance we meet, get us closer to our life's *mission*, our *destiny*. At the time, I didn't know the significance of why I was so heavily driven to keep a promise made so lightly. I had spent most of my life wondering what I was doing on earth, confused. My spirit must have known that this promise would illuminate a truth just one breadcrumb shy of the ultimate reason I existed.

Before this wedding, I never really believed I could keep a promise when it came to the love of another. Romance had eluded me and I was certain that this promise would unravel the love and patience Gerard had for me. But this turned out to be a "spirit promise." Spirit promises are those that you are driven to keep, by the demand of your soul, no matter the cost and resistance. These promises surface clearly on the ripples of an otherwise murky life, to reflect your true nature back to you. They are different from circumstantial promises, which are made on the fly and easily forgotten.

When you make a promise and then find yourself motivated to keep it, you are on track to learn your whole, big, and awesome purpose. Your desire to fulfill a promise is like God talking to you. There is a sense of urgency to fulfilling these spirit promises. Look for those you are driven to make good on, then follow the steps right to the center of them. Spirit promises transcend changing circumstances to uphold our higher truth.

Look back through your life for the promises you have been motivated to keep. Each one you have fulfilled holds within it a clue to your purpose on earth. Every clue you need is right before you; surrendering to your promises allows your purpose to spring forth and illuminate your path.

Exercise: Promise Power

1. Make a list of five to ten promises you have made and have been highly motivated to keep.

2. Look for three or more promises in life that meant the world for you to keep.

3. For each of those three, answer these questions: How did you feel when you fulfilled it? What did you discover about yourself through the act of fulfilling it?

4. Now answer these questions: What is similar about each promise? What is similar about how you felt when you fulfilled each one?

5. Pick a word from the similarities you see in your kept promises. Perhaps it's to inspire, enjoy, heal, nurture, or be happy. Whatever it is will give you a very big clue to your purpose, your destiny.

Finally, you come to the place where your soul asks to be heard. By reflecting on the promises you hold dear, your mission can make itself known and thus your love can take flight. When you surrender to your mission, allowing it to guide your relationships—in business, love, and all of life—everything starts to make sense. Your purpose is hidden in plain sight, in the promises you keep.

When you are aligned with your purpose, driven by it, you might be potentially harder to handle for some, but the right people will be drawn to you. When you are aligned with your heart's mission, you are given gifts, support, love, and tools to achieve the tasks at hand. It's then up to you to accept the gifts, releasing your fears to the fires that will diminish them—allowing for love to come to you, burning away the doubts, filling you with the ability to serve.

> Love is a promise, love is a souvenir, once given
> never forgotten, never let it disappear.
>
> —JOHN LENNON

17

Generosity Eliminates Fear

A Cup of Giving

*Real generosity toward the future lies in
giving all to the present.*

—ALBERT CAMUS

Inspiration: Ambrosia Plum is an effervescent, peony-style white tea from Sri Lanka that sparkles on the tongue, with subtle hints of strawberries grown in ocean air, jammy, summer-ripe plum, sweet stevia leaves from rich Uruguayan soil, and a dash of rose petals for goodwill. It is a cup of what is possible—giving our mouths and minds that shaky but intoxicating slight drunkenness we get from taking the first step just beyond our comfort zone. Visions of sugarplums and dancing fairies are sometimes seen while sipping this blend of future dreams made real.

In the twelfth century, Chinese emperor Hui Zong fell so deeply in love with the delicate beauty of white tea that he would eventually lose his empire over it. Back then, the royal court allowed only the fairest virgins—using sterling silver bird-shaped scissors—to clip the pure, bright tea buds that grew on the white-as-snow bushes. Coveted by all other tea-drinking nations, particularly England, white tea was so precious it was reserved for royal lips. It was rumored that in rare intimate moments, the royals would allow their concubines to sip the nectar from their mouths as foreplay and with the promise of eternal youth.

Dedicated tea masters took the cuttings to other parts of the world, in the hope of being able to grow this prized white tea for themselves. Its cultivation was mastered on the island of Sri Lanka, high up in the mountains in Gnana's biodynamic estate, even though they had been told they could not grow white tea there, that it could be cultivated only by the tea cultivars of Fujian province, China. But after decades of patiently attempting and failing, they refined their approach and perfected their own white-peony-style teas. The envy of tea growers everywhere, it tastes like a subtle symphony of honey, fruit, rain collected from jasmine flowers, and a hint of innocence.

It is very difficult to grow and carefully process the precious Chinese-style teas that have taken thousands of years to perfect in faraway lands. A tea this refined and delicate requires the tea maker to honor time, meditative patience, focus, and thoughtful effort. It cannot be rushed. It's a style of leaf made of mindfulness. The process of trial and error is a luxury rarely gifted to tea makers, but the same patience that it took to transform a desolate tea estate into a thriving biodynamic, fair-trade tea garden would inspire Gnana and the estate owners to carry out this long-term vision of careful cultivation. They make white teas as fine as the Chinese do, green teas as pure as the mountain air, and beautiful, distinct hand-tied blooming teas fit for transformational, life-affirming tea rituals.

With each visit to Gnana's estate, I tasted their precious teas as they developed them. They created a universe of tea in one boutique garden. In the tasting room on the top floor of the factory, I looked over the mountains above the tea fields where they grow their artisan-crafted teas. They are generous and conscientious—taking time to develop people, land, and the rare arts that cherish human efforts. Here I found my spiritual family, a partner for my tea company, and married my soul mate.

With my annual visits to this estate and its beautiful people, my relationship to them grew organically. When Sage turned eleven, his health had improved enough to venture on the long journey with me. We headed for the sacred realm together, excited to be delivering a trunk full of donated and restored laptop computers for the estate-run computer learning center that educates the tea workers' children. Neesa, Gnana's assistant, had been one of the first graduates of the center, and she was helping Gnana modernize the systems so that handwritten ledgers could become automated—giving him more time for developing new social programs and precious new teas.

I had been struck by the ancient artistry required to make these fine teas contrasted with the fast technology Gnana brought to the children through the computer learning center he had built for their education. It could take one worker up to twenty minutes to produce one cup of the hand-tied white teas, which took training and time, along with a desire to master the art and stay in the rural, tea-producing community. If the 530 children on the estate all went through the computer learning center and graduated, how many of them would want to stay in the country and spend long hours hand-tying these teas? My guess—from watching Sage speed into the future via his keyboard—was very few. Whom would we pass the artisan tea-making torch to? But like Gnana, I loved seeing the children's excited faces and confident smiles as they mastered new computer skills, and also like Gnana, I wanted to help enable more of this in any way I could. I feared the estate would be abandoned and this beautiful utopia lost, buried underneath the promise of quickness through technology, but I still wanted every child to learn technology and be empowered by it. Even though I had an aching worry that all of the children might one day leave for the cities to find technology jobs and abandon the arts of fine tea making, I knew there had to be something I wasn't seeing, a solution already thought through by Gnana. Was it possible to have our tea and technology, too? This estate had become my lifeline in so many ways, showing me what was possible, and I never wanted it to be forgotten or lost as the world sped up in the name of technological progress.

As Sage and I headed up to the tea-growing region from Colombo, our car clung to a pencil-thin track that fell away on one side in a thousand-foot drop. I kept an arm around Sage, whose face had gone white, making his freckles stand out. His green eyes were huge as the driver expertly dodged elephants, dogs, orange-robed Buddhist monks on motorcycles, entire families crammed seven to a little motor-powered tuk-tuk, and barefoot children walking to school with their books hugged closely to their chests. After so many trips to the estate, I was used to the death-defying drive.

"Almost there, kiddo," I told him, patting his shoulder. "You're going to love it."

In preparation for visiting the computer lab, I told Sage about the five schools that served all 530 children on the estate, and about the one computer learning lab.

"Sage, the computer learning center can only seat about ten kids at a time, so that's why we're bringing our friends' donated laptops to them. The idea is to allow the kids to check them out like library books—take them home and do their assignments, and then we'll be able to open the training up so that all the kids can have access to it."

I told Sage about Durga, one of the first children to benefit from the schools and computer lab. She was graduating soon and choosing a college. My eyes watered with emotion as I thought of this beautiful, eager child I met at age eight, who later had sat next to Gerard and me on our wedding day, and who'd now grown into a spirited young woman.

"Sage, if you were living on a farm that took a lot of hard work, would you want to stay there to be in nature, or would you want to take your computer skills and move to a city?" I asked.

"Mom, I don't know. I'm more worried about falling off this cliff."

"These kids, they're going off to college and careers. They won't want to stay on the estate. And then their parents will retire and . . ."

Sage dug his fingernails into my forearm as we miraculously scraped by a bus piled high with commuters. I remembered my first drive out to the estate. When I had begged the driver to slow down, he had smiled proudly at me in the rearview mirror. "Oh, Madam, this is how we get everywhere in our country."

When I had arrived at the estate all those years ago, it had felt like I had come home. After swerving for hours on the treacherous mountain road with my life flashing across the back of my clenched eyelids, I opened them to waterfalls cutting through mountains and stately smiling Buddhas towering over glimmering domed temples. Upon waking up the following morning in a colonial-era room to a pot of simmering black tea with warm raw milk and sticky brown sugar swirling in the white porcelain cup, it had all melted away—the thirty-plus plane hours, whole-day layovers in Dubai and Bangkok, hectic airport transfers, hours of stomach-twisting car rides to Colombo. From where I lay, looking up at the long baroque curtains—all my worries about money, my son's health challenges, being in over my head and overwhelmed—seemed manageable. I felt sure it would all come to good. My heart swelled with the beauty of this country and its people.

Sri Lanka is like a small island version of India with extra-good manners and nearly a 100 percent literacy rate. School is free and accessible to most. The island mentality of waste not, want not simmers to the top of each person's attitude toward life; consumption lags in a good way.

Sri Lanka produces the hottest and sweetest cinnamon, deliciously round-bodied black tea leaves, and pungent spices: cloves, pink and black peppercorns, cardamom, and ginger. The handiwork is so thoughtful, so specialized and accomplished, that some of the world's finest lingerie is made there. And the food, oh that *food*, is such a culinary delight that every person who goes there dreams of golden curries and string hoppers (a spaghetti pancake!) the rest of their days.

"What if . . . ," I fretted, as we pulled up to the small guesthouse where Sage and I were to stay in Haputale, the village near the tea estate. "What if all of the beautiful, organic, biodynamic, handmade teas are lost because there is no one here to pass the hard-earned craft to? There is no machine that can make them. It would be a great loss to the world, like losing champagne. The only difference is that champagne fetches enough money to make it lucrative—the growers and winemakers are incentivized by money in exchange for their artistry. Tea is still so undervalued, what if we don't have enough time to educate people to pay more and these teas are . . ."

I was jarred out of my preoccupation when my son punched me in the arm.

"Ow! Sage! What's that for?"

"I could have *died* on that road!" he huffed and slammed the car door.

I knew it wouldn't be long before the place worked its magic on him. And sure enough, the next day found him in fevered conversations with the students at the school about his favorite things: computers, software, video games, code, and math. He couldn't believe how much they knew about Windows OS, Photoshop, website design, and programming, and he happily told them everything he could about technology and pop culture outside the realm of their remote tea fields.

Gnana sat with me as we ate string hopper, dal, and spicy coconut chutney with our hands. Once we'd caught up on all that had happened in the six months since we'd seen each other, I put my worry before Gnana.

"What's going to happen when the children go to university and leave the estate? Who will move in to dedicate their lives to the craft of plucking and making the tea?" I felt almost embarrassed to have this sort of worry when I was responsible for helping them get out of the tea fields through the fair-trade programs I'd made a cornerstone of my company. It felt like I was cheating a bit on my own mission, looking at my own business and selfishly wondering who would pluck the tea when the tea workers graduated from college and became software engineers, a dream that Durga had shyly whispered to me on my last visit, her big brown eyes holding back hopeful tears.

Gnana stopped eating, and in his calm Buddha-like way, he smiled broadly. "Oh, Zheeeena, remember that those who can see the invisible can do the impossible, yes?"

I nodded as I savored an extra-spicy mouthful of dal-soaked hopper.

"Well, you see," he said, "we have a plan."

Gnana is the closest person I know to a true holy man. His big-joy smiles and curious deep eyes are always a beacon of serenity and equanimity.

Gnana sees all beings as sentient and worthy of compassion, fairness, and friendship. The owners of the estate are the same. It had been so unlikely it was deemed impossible for a group of financial partners to invest in a visionary project like this. I wondered now how they would feel about the risks at hand—that the very project funded by their generosity over the years could potentially create a generational cliff that could cost them their legacy.

The owners had been told they'd never succeed taking the abandoned estate, which had become a barren plot of high-altitude soil, and making it grow high-yielding, super-immune plants that would produce golden liquors without using pesticides and commercial fertilizers, but they did. They were told that the impoverished locals would never become productive workers, but they did. The owners were told that the price tag on their lofty vision would be too steep, but they held the long-term ideal of sustainability, the craft of the world's finest and rarest artisan teas, and worker rights, and so today it is the shining example of what is possible. They looked over the weak, struggling tea bushes, the stripped soil, the tilted workers' shanties, and the depressed workers who were used to a poverty so deep they knew daily hunger and staggering infant mortality rates. Anyone else would have seen the impossibility, but, as Gnana says, they saw the "invisible."

They fed the stripped soil. They also fed the people and gave them houses, health care, and built clean water systems. They gave the children books, schools, music, and art and empowered them, ensuring they were taught no fear, so that they wouldn't be limited to the same life but would be able to see the invisible for themselves.

Gnana refilled my teacup and smiled into my worried face.

"Yes, we want the children to go away to university," he said. "And like you, we wondered what would happen if we got what we wanted—a totally educated, upwardly mobile generation of children. We wondered how we would offer them something they would value enough to bring their knowledge back home. I have discussed this opportunity with the owners of the estate, and we have decided to do something that has never been done before in this country."

I leaned in, eager to hear.

"We are going to give the workers the land." He sat back in his bamboo chair, smiling.

"Give them the land?" I repeated. "How will that work?"

"In this way: Each family will become landowners of their own section of the estate. They will grow tea and will have to run their farm like a business, using the skills they learn in the computer lab, in school, and in biodynamic farming," Gnana said. "We will buy the tea from them and process it in the factory as we currently do. You see, this gives them total autonomy and makes them small-business owners. They like the idea of added responsibility very much indeed. It's a challenge, and they love to learn."

Once again, this beacon of a tea garden, so remote and hidden from most of the world, had revealed itself to be a light in the face of fear, scarcity, and limits. Making each worker a landowner was a leap of faith that could revolutionize the way large tea estates are run one day. The estate owners were giving away their investment; it was a breathtaking leap of faith.

"Let me tell you a story," he said. "Once, in the beginning of our ownership here, there was a worker who wanted to become a barber. We sent him to school to learn his trade and then he returned and opened a barbershop right in the middle of the tea estate. Now he cuts hair here for all of the workers, and his salon is a community gathering place. He could have gone to any city, but he wanted to come back to be of service here. We didn't expect it; it was by his free will that he came back to share his gifts and talents with us."

I asked, "So maybe the children like Durga will learn these advanced computer skills and come back here to develop programs for other children?"

"Maybe so, but that is up to them as individuals. It's by their free will. We do not give in order to get a return."

We ate in silence for a few minutes as this sank in for me. Again, I was reminded of the Sikhs' serving food outside of the

Golden Temple, who gave for the sake of giving, rather than for the sake of saving or feeling self-important.

He continued, "On another occasion, there was a worker who wanted to become a psychologist, and we found a way to send him to school. He could have gone anywhere to practice his therapy afterward, but he came back to become a social worker here, to help our people, his people, deal with social challenges—he did this from his heart. We find that by giving opportunity without any expectation, we receive not only the gifts of doing what is right but also unexpected gifts as these.

"You see, Zheeena, if you are fearless in your giving, you will find there is actually nothing to fear."

"This has the power to transform the world," I said to him. Our eyes met and he smiled in his thoughtful way.

Generosity Eliminates Fear

Mantra of the Cup: I give generously and all my needs and wants are fulfilled effortlessly.

When you are fearful of not having enough money, give some away. When you are feeling unattractive, notice someone else's beauty and compliment her on it. If you are stressed out about not having enough time, donate some. When you are feeling like no one cares about you, care for others—set up a day for yourself to go and volunteer for a cause that matters to you or offer some time to listen to a friend. Money will come back to you, beauty will arrive, time will expand, and caring will be yours.

But know the difference between charity and generosity. Charity is often to help others in need, while generosity is to help others from a place of giving for the sake of giving. To be generous is a constant practice, while being charitable is an occasional practice expressed when someone is in need.

Gnana taught me the antidote to fear. Through his example of fearless generosity, he inspired me to become a better person, and also granted me permission to dream even bigger every time I thought I would fail. I owe his team—his workers, teachers, and fair-trade officers—the utmost gratitude for creating a heaven on earth and for making fine tea that is infused with love for me to share with customers across the globe. From that first crate of tea that arrived quietly from his garden, to today, the hints of the leaves led me to him and have in turn given me a purpose.

Many years ago, I was told the story about angels and demons. When reflecting on how to illuminate the power of giving and the power of service, this tale surfaced in my heart to share with you.

Once upon a time, God set up an elaborate feast for a group of angels in one room and an equally elaborate feast for a group of demons in another. There was every kind of delicacy: dates and figs drizzled with golden honey, pears baked with the butter of sacred milk, delicate white teas grown on Mt. Olympus, fish from the lakes of heaven, and wines made of the afterworld's rarest grapes.

God entered each room and explained the one rule of the feast, "You may feast and the food will replenish, you may drink and the wine shall be a flowing fountain of never-ending libation. The feast is endless, the food nourishing and delicious, it is the finest delicacy of all heaven served to you." He paused before adding, "There is only one, very simple rule . . ."

Both the angels and demons leaned in to listen more closely, and God said, "You cannot bend your elbows to eat. You must keep your arms straight."

With that, God closed the door to each feasting room and left.

Hours later, God returned to check on the angels and demons, and from outside the doors, he heard the demons arguing and fighting. He opened the door and not one bite of the feast had been taken, as each time a demon tried to take a bite, he couldn't reach his mouth without bending his elbows. They were so mad; all they could do was yell and scream at one another.

God shook his head and closed the door as he stepped back into the hallway. They hadn't even noticed he had reappeared, as they were blind with hunger and rage. This would go on for an eternity.

In contrast, as God approached the angels' door, he heard lilting laughter and soft singing. He quietly opened to the door and peered into the banquet room. The angels were feeding and serving wine to one another with straight arms, and the food was glittering and glowing in divine love while they feasted, laughing and chatting between mouthfuls.

God smiled. Obviously, the angels got it.

There is no higher purpose or honor in anyone's life than to serve and nourish others. May your days be filled with this knowing.

Go forth in the direction of your heart's desire. May these lessons, stories, exercises, and prayers bring you comfort and joy. Remember them when you are hiking the trail of your destiny.

Always believe in the magic your gifts have to brighten the dark night when change is howling at your window. Allow your light to illuminate others' paths as you feel your way toward your personal, brilliant purpose. Inspire others by serving them. Carve, ask, show up, seek blessings, generate gratitude, remain steady in your heart, celebrate your niche, collaborate with others, stay curious, celebrate successes, appreciate and validate, allow others' kindnesses to fill your cup, allow your spirit to make promises your heart keeps, and remember that there is no better cure for any woe than generosity. May your journey be blessed as you travel the rim of your very own life by the cup.

Host Your Own Gypsy Tea Party

A Cup of Celebration

The more you praise and celebrate your life,
the more there is in life to celebrate.

—OPRAH WINFREY

In the old country, women arrived in caravans for a tea party. They pulled their painted wagons into a tight circle in the golden field of wildflowers. Bells tinkled, incense smoke rose, and children laughed. A creek ran close by, and the Mistress of Tea would collect the freshwater in her copper kettle for tea. The tribe of women hung garlands from one wagon to the next, and from the garlands hung tins once used for tea and now filled with scented candles to illuminate the gathering.

Women ran from wagon to wagon, lifting their layered skirts as they climbed the steps. They shared their jewels, dressed each other in silks and embroidered corsets, draped intricately stitched shawls across their shoulders. A sparkling jewel was placed in the center of their foreheads, signifying a spiritual event, symbolizing their sight would be that of the higher mind, not just that of their two eyes. They mixed essential oils and patted white patchouli, lilac, and osmanthus perfume on their pulse points. They wore rings on their toes, flowers in their hair, and sparkles on their skin.

The Mistress of Tea called for them as the sun began to set and the sky became pink. She called to her sisters, her tribe, and announced the tea party had begun. The circle of women clapped, hugged each other, and took in the visual delights. There was a table filled with sensual treats of tea-infused desserts, glass teapots glimmered over small candles, and the scents of bergamot, jasmine, lavender, and rose swirled through the air, mingling with the sweet laughter and lilting voices.

Adorned and smiling, the circle of women sipped the aromatic tea from mismatched teacups collected over many years. They gave thanks to Mother Earth and sent a prayer to the women whose hands so carefully plucked the tea leaves. Women of a Gypsy Tea Party are mindful, transcending life's daily toils for the celebration of their divine deliciousness.

As I stepped into my role as Mistress of Tea, bringing Gypsy Tea Parties into the world, I discovered that there is a Mistress of Tea in all of us. It's in our nature to be wondrous, fiery, feminine, passionate, and present. As Mistress of Tea, I have thrown tea parties all over the United States, Canada, and even Iceland. The formula I found that works best encourages the attendees to express their inner Gypsy—their creative soul that might not get to come out very often in their daily life.

One of my most memorable Gypsy Tea Parties was at ABC Carpet & Home in New York City. It was for Eve Ensler's Broadway play *The Good Body*, in which she comes to terms with her body and makes peace with it through reconnecting with her stomach. To illuminate the play's powerful message, I brought in belly dancers of every shape, size, age, race, and level of fitness to perform and celebrate the female essence in all of its diverse beauty. PURE Bellydance troupe fit the bill and performed and taught us all about our deeply personal beauty. Hundreds of women attended.

We sipped tea, listened to storytellers, and learned a belly dance that we all performed in a huge circle. We wrote love notes to our bodies and hung them on a tree that rose in the middle of the room, in the spirit of "loving your tree."

The art of belly dancing was never meant to be viewed by men; it was a shared art among women that helped them prepare for and then heal from childbirth. It goes perfectly with a cup of tea. Belly dancing burns away the ego while tea relaxes the mind and the circle of sisterhood is strengthened.

Hosting a Gypsy Tea Party gives you a chance to celebrate your creativity and the friendship you share with your "tribe." It's also a means for you to shine and be the Mistress of Tea for the event. Don your best boho-chic garb, pile on the sparkling makeup, and prepare your own bountiful gathering of feminine splendor!

You can host a Gypsy Tea Party for any occasion—a book club, a baby or bridal shower, a birthday party, a bachelorette party, or simply as a means to get together with your friends. I have thrown them as super-successful fund-raisers for causes like V-Day.

When I was a lonely single mom, the tea parties not only launched my business and sparked my creative flame but also drew others into my life in an authentic way. Sharing tea and stories, empowerment exercises, and delicious foods with others brings you closer together. A Gypsy Tea Party is a fun way to express yourself and give your circle of friends a chance to do the same.

Elements of a Gypsy Tea Party

Invitations. Handwritten invitations are a beautiful touch for your gathering. I use Sugarcube Press's handmade cards for mine. I love their cards with the henna tattooed hands, so exotic and elegant—perfect for a Gypsy Tea Party invitation. You can make your own on card stock, or maybe use paper and roll it into a scroll, mailing it out in tubes. Or if you have time you can even hand-deliver them yourself, as the Mistress of Tea. I suggest mailing them at least a month in advance. Indicate that this is a dress-up event with a Gypsy theme.

Adornments. As the Mistress of Tea, you can provide bindis (a small adhesive jewel usually worn on the forehead) at the door—I like to let my friends pick their own when they arrive. It adds a nice mystical touch of ritual to the event. Also, either ask the attendees to bring scarves or provide them at the door. I love the scarves that have coins on the ends that jingle; the sound of hips swaying with the coins is beautiful. I also like sparkles, lots of them, so I usually have a small tray of skin sparkles for my friends to paint onto their arms, chests, hands, and feet—like fairy dust for big girls!

Décor. Christmas lights, paper lanterns, fresh-cut flowers (in empty Gypsy Tea tins!), and candles (tea lights) all add to the vibe of the Gypsy lifestyle. Incense and bright silky pillows and throws strewn about create a lounge effect in any room. I use floor pillows, low tables, and Moroccan poufs; it's more fun when people are lounging on the floor like in an exotic teahouse.

Teapots and teacups. Ask your guests to bring their favorite teacup, and if they don't have one, offer plenty for them to choose from. I buy one at a time, never matching, and love to see which ones my friends gravitate to. A fun practice is to have your guests share the story of their favorite teacup. I comb antique stores for teapots and cups, and also love the ones they sell at Anthropologie. I have lots of resources for teapots and teacups at www.Zhena.tv.

Flower arrangements. When my yard is in bloom, I use iceberg roses, jasmine, lavender, rosemary, sage, orange blossoms, lemon verbena, and hibiscus for my arrangements. Wherever you live, try to use wildflowers if they are in season or buy cut flowers and design your own arrangements. It's been scientifically proven that people who look at flowers are happier. Get creative and don't hold back on the use of color! I use my empty tea tins as vases, but you can use anything from a vase to a canning jar. It's all up to you!

Entertainment. Musicians, belly dancers, tarot or tea leaf readers, and henna artists are all great options for your Gypsy Tea Party. I have held big tea parties with all the entertainment under the sun and also have had very small, intimate gatherings with no entertainment that were still a great success. As the Mistress of Tea, you can decide what you want the vibe to be. Classical or Spanish guitarists make for more mellow affairs; Middle Eastern tabla players go with belly dancing.

If you hire a tarot, palm, or tea leaf reader, ensure she is super positive and spiritual. I read palms, so I like to do these myself at my events, but before I hire readers I get a reading from them to make sure they are good. Uplifting, insightful, and joyful are the prerequisites.

I recommend hiring a belly dancer who can teach your guests a small routine, which the group can perform together. For most of my events, I hire my former belly dance instructor, Beth Amine, who is also a teacher and performer. She makes all the women laugh and feel comfortable in their bodies. Remember, this is for women to break down their stresses into laughs, not a competition about who can shimmy the best.

Empowerment. There is one rule with the Gypsy Tea Party: No gossip and no negativity or negative language. The conversations should be centered on spirituality, love, ideas, hopes, dreams, and gratitude. Keep it positive and empowering for everyone. Using the exercises in this book is a great way to ensure your tea party is transformative for your guests.

The sharing circle. After the belly-dancing lesson, I usually have a sharing circle where I ask each friend about something she really wants to do in life, about a dream she has. I usually start out and share one of my dreams, for example, "I want to take my mom to Italy." Then, as the Mistress of Tea, you facilitate a question or two, such as, "Is there anything you need from us to help you make that happen?" Just getting the chance to say a dream out loud starts bringing it closer to reality. Also, you can use this book, and the questions at the end of each chapter, to spark a sharing circle. Make sure everyone has a chance to talk, and if it's a bigger crowd you may want to playfully use a timer to have time for everyone. There are more ideas and worksheets at www .Zhena.tv.

Gifts. I love to give tea to everyone. I usually take a tin of tea, wrap raffia around it with flowers and herbs from my yard, and then give one to all the women as their gifts for attending. You can give anything you want, just make sure to give something with a handmade touch so that they have a token of your affection to carry home after your wonderful offering of a transcendent experience. Life gets busy, and the calm, happy celebration of your Gypsy Tea Party will be a fond memory for your friends. Your gift is their touchstone to remember it by.

Menu. Vary the flavors at your tea party: spice, sweet, salty, and playful. Match desserts with teas; use local honey and a variety of milks to create creamy libations. I like to use my dear friend Ted Dennard's Tupelo honey drizzled on Brie and fresh berries for an easy gourmet treat with little effort. Also, my friend and recipe developer for baked goods, Kate, has developed some lovely recipes included here for you to use.

There are many more "Baker and Tea Maker" tea-infused recipes at www.Zhena.tv. Feel free to browse them to make your very own menu. Included here are some fabulous and surprisingly simple recipes for you to dazzle your friends with!

Tea Party Recipes

Rise and Shine Black Tea Latte

ea lattes are easy to make at home and require no special equipment. You can find gourmet syrups at almost any grocery store or online. I love the salty-sweet complexity of salted caramel syrup with my Bed and Breakfast black tea for a special treat (like when I've been a good girl at the gym!). There are hundreds of variations on a theme when it comes to tea lattes, so get creative and allow your inner tea mistress to shine.

> 1 Zhena's Bed and Breakfast or other breakfast black tea sachet,
>   or 1 teaspoon loose tea
> 6 ounces milk (I use soy, but you can use dairy, almond, oat, or
>   even rice milk; this recipe doesn't taste as good with coconut
>   or hemp milk.)
> 1 ounce salted caramel syrup or sauce (I like Torani syrup. It's
>   a San Francisco–based family-owned business with a female
>   CEO!)
> Pink Himalayan salt to sprinkle on top
> Whipped cream, optional (not ultra-pasteurized; it doesn't whip)

Espresso machine:

Steep the tea sachet or loose tea in 2 ounces of boiling water for 3 minutes. This creates a tea "espresso."

Steam the milk.

Combine the tea "espresso" with the steamed milk and the syrup. Add foam on top and then a sprinkle of pink Himalayan salt. Enjoy.

Stovetop:

In a saucepan over medium-high heat, simmer the tea sachet or loose tea and the milk until the desired temperature has been reached, approximately 4–5 minutes.

Remove the tea sachet or strain the leaves.

Stir in the syrup.

Sprinkle Himalayan pink salt on top, or enjoy as is.

Gypsy Rose Flourless Dark Chocolate Cake

This gluten-free cake is sensual and opens one's heart to romance and authenticity. Kate has been making this for her darling husband for years, and it never fails to delight. I love this with a big pot of Gypsy Rose tea simply as is, no milk or honey. I drink the elegant rose tea with the mysterious and smoky black tea base and take small bites of this cake. You can watch the video on our YouTube page (www.youtube.com/zhenamuzyka) for instruction and some lighthearted banter when I learned to bake this in Kate's beautiful bakery on the beach in Ventura, California.

> 10 ounces fair-trade-certified dark chocolate, broken into pieces
> 6 ounces unsalted butter, or coconut oil at room temperature for a vegan option
> 2 Zhena's Gypsy Rose tea sachets
> 6 eggs at room temperature, or egg substitute
> ½ cup sugar
> 2 teaspoons vanilla extract ("double vanilla," from a gourmet store, is even better!)
> ½ cup unsweetened cocoa powder

Preheat the oven to 325°.

Lightly grease a 9-inch springform pan with oil or butter.

Place 3 inches of water in the bottom of a double boiler and let it come to a boil. Reduce the heat so the water is at a slow boil, then put the chocolate into the top pan. Do not stir for 5 minutes.

While the chocolate is heating, melt the butter or oil in a small pan and empty the tea sachets into it. Steep for 5 minutes.

Strain the "tea butter" through a tea strainer into the melted chocolate and whisk together. Remove from the heat when the mixture is smooth.

Add the eggs, sugar, vanilla, and cocoa, and mix until smooth.

Pour the batter into the cake pan and bake for 45–55 minutes.

Cool completely and then refrigerate for 4–24 hours before serving, depending on how firm you want the consistency.

To serve, add a chocolate syrup design on top, and if you really want to impress your lover or friends, add fresh red rose petals or rosebuds—make sure they aren't sprayed with chemicals, of course. ☺

Serve with Gypsy Rose black tea or port wine. Yum.

Makes 8 slices.

Sumptuous Peach-Ginger-Infused Scones

K ate bakes the most exquisite scones at her bakery. There is nothing better than a peach-ginger-infused scone, with some lemon curd or just warm butter, and a big mug of Peach Ginger tea with milk and honey. This recipe welcomes you to the land of limitless possibilities.

1½ cups self-rising flour, sifted
⅓ cup sugar
3 ounces cold salted butter
1 Zhena's Peach Ginger tea sachet, or 1 teaspoon loose tea
1 cup cold milk

Preheat the oven to 350°.

In a food processor, pulse the flour, sugar, butter, and tea from the sachet until the butter is broken up into very small pieces.

Place the mixture in a large bowl and slowly add the milk, stirring very well between additions. Add only enough milk to make the scone mixture come together.

Sprinkle some flour on your counter and knead the mixture until the dough comes together, usually 1–2 minutes. Do not overknead, as this will create a "tough" scone. Press down the dough until it is about 1 inch thick. Cut the dough into 6 triangles. Don't worry about being precise—one of the charms of scones is that they look like loving hands, not a machine, made them.

Place the scones on a parchment-lined baking sheet and bake for 15–18 minutes, until the tops are golden.

Let the scones cool for 5 minutes and then serve.

Makes 6 scones.

Raspberry Earl Grey Chocolate Cupcakes

*W*hen Kate and I were baking these, we were giddy with chocolate, rum, and the happy scent of raspberries and Bergamot. These make amazing birthday cupcakes—Sage loves them! Frost with Raspberry Earl Grey Dark Chocolate Rum Icing (recipe below); you can top them with a fresh raspberry and chocolate shavings to make them even more beautiful. Serve with Raspberry Earl Grey or Bed and Breakfast black tea and enjoy the spirit of collaboration—in much the way these recipes were born.

> 3 eggs at room temperature
> ¾ cup sugar
> ¾ cup unsalted butter, softened
> 1 cup all-purpose flour
> ⅓ cup unsweetened cocoa powder
> 1 teaspoon baking powder
> 1 teaspoon vanilla extract

Preheat the oven to 325°.

With an electric mixer, beat the eggs and sugar together until doubled in volume. This should take 3–5 minutes.

Set the mixer on low and mix in the butter. Then add the vanilla and mix at medium-high for 1 minute.

Sift together the flour, cocoa, and baking powder. Slowly add the dry ingredients to the batter and mix on low until incorporated. Stir now and then with a spatula until all the dry ingredients are incorporated.

Line a muffin pan with cupcake liners and fill each cup ⅔ full.

Bake for 18–20 minutes.

Frost with Raspberry Earl Grey Dark Chocolate Rum Icing.

Makes 12 cupcakes.

Raspberry Earl Grey Dark Chocolate Rum Icing

*T*his decadent frosting perfectly tops the delicious cupcakes. It has just a little rum, enough for flavor, but if you are sensitive to alcohol, you can use nonalcoholic rum extract instead. There's something magical about the combination of chocolate, raspberry, and rum—three very different flavors that collaborate for a party in your mouth!

½ cup unsweetened, dark cocoa powder, preferably organic and fair-trade certified
1 Zhena's Raspberry Earl Grey black tea sachet
½ pound unsalted butter, softened
3 cups confectioners' sugar
3 tablespoons dark rum, or 1 teaspoon rum extract
3 tablespoons milk
½ teaspoon raspberry extract
Milk

Mix together the cocoa and the tea leaves in a large bowl.
Add the butter and mix until smooth and creamy.
Mix in the confectioners' sugar and then slowly add the rum and raspberry extract. Mix for 3–5 minutes on medium high. If the icing looks dry, add ½ teaspoon of milk at a time, mixing well between additions. Scrape down the sides of the icing and stir.
Use a piping bag or a pastry knife to ice the cupcakes.

Makes enough to frost 12 cupcakes.

Coconut Chai–Infused French Macaroons with Raspberry Earl Grey Dark Chocolate Ganache

*H*ere's where I admit a favorite. These macaroons bring so much delight by themselves, and with the amazing addition of the chocolate ganache, there is nothing like them. Kate brought these to the tea company headquarters when she was formulating her recipes for her bakery—really when it was still a dream without a location. Now she serves these best-selling morsels to hundreds of her devotees a week, I among them!

> 1½ cups almond flour
> 2 cups confectioners' sugar
> 1 Zhena's Coconut Chai tea sachet
> 4 egg whites at room temperature
> Pinch cream of tartar
> ½ cup granulated sugar

Sift together the almond flour and confectioners' sugar. Stir in the tea leaves and mix thoroughly. Set aside.

With an electric mixer, whip the egg whites with the cream of tartar until soft peaks form. Sprinkle in the granulated sugar and beat the egg whites until they are glossy and stiff peaks form.

One-third at a time, fold the almond mixture into the egg whites.

Line two baking sheets with parchment paper. Pour the batter into a pastry bag and pipe out small half circles 1 inch apart.

Let the cookies sit on the counter for 30 minutes or until their tops have formed a dry skin. Halfway through the waiting time, preheat the oven to 325°.

Bake the cookies for 12–15 minutes. Let them cool completely before removing them from the parchment.

Makes 20 cookies.

Raspberry Earl Grey Dark Chocolate Ganache Filling for Coconut Chai Macaroons

*W*e use Raspberry Earl Grey for this ganache, but you can use Egyptian Mint, which lifts and cools the spices in the chai macaroons, or any other green or black tea. I always love the result of an unexpected flavor combination; synergy and delight come from taking risks!

½ cup whipping cream
1 Zhena's Raspberry Earl Grey tea sachet
4 ounces chocolate (milk, dark, bittersweet, or semisweet), broken into pieces
1 tablespoon unsalted butter

In a small skillet, simmer the whipping cream and the contents of the tea sachet over a low flame for 5 minutes.

Strain the cream over the chocolate and let sit for 5 minutes before stirring.

Stir well, and when completely smooth, add the butter and mix again.

One by one, remove a macaroon from the parchment and dip the flat bottom in the chocolate and place it on the flat side of another cookie, making a cookie sandwich. Now dip the cookie into the chocolate. Place the cookies on parchment to cool.

Makes 20 macaroons.

Caramel Chai Panna Cotta (Gluten Free)

*T*his is a decadent celebration of cream, Caramel Chai, and simplicity. Enjoy it as a reward for all you do in the world, and remember to always celebrate each success in order for the universe to keep 'em coming! You can make this recipe with vegan gelatin replacement and coconut milk along with nondairy yogurt for a vegan version.

    1 envelope (1 tablespoon) gelatin
    2 tablespoons cool water in a small bowl
    1 cup whipping cream
    ⅓ cup sugar
    2 Zhena's Caramel Chai tea sachets
    17 ounces plain Greek yogurt

Sprinkle the gelatin over the water and set aside.

In a small pan, heat the cream, sugar, and tea over medium-low heat for 5 minutes. Stir frequently.

Remove the tea mixture from the heat. Add the gelatin and whisk until it fully dissolves.

Place the yogurt in a large bowl and strain in the tea mixture. Mix well.

Pour into ramekins and refrigerate for 8–16 hours. Serve cold.

Makes 6 4-ounce servings.

Blueberry Vanilla Green Darjeeling Tea Ice Cream

Although our natures are exposed when we are in "hot water," cool, refreshing ice cream can be the perfect comfort food when we need comforting the most. I love the perfect floral astringency of Darjeeling green tea, and the sweet antioxidant boost of the blueberries balances perfectly with creamy vanilla. Enjoy this alone or with Gypsy Rose Flourless Dark Chocolate Cake, an amazing combination! Note that this recipe requires an ice cream maker.

2 cups milk (you can also use nondairy options)
1 cup fresh blueberries
Seeds from 2 vanilla beans
2 tablespoons loose-leaf Darjeeling green tea
2 cups whipping cream
1 cup sugar
1 tablespoon vanilla extract

In a medium pot, place 2 cups of milk, the blueberries, and the vanilla bean seeds, and heat on medium-low until small rolling bubbles from. Add the tea and turn off the heat. Let the tea infuse for 30 minutes and then strain and refrigerate overnight.

The next day, in a mixing bowl, whisk 2 cups of milk, the cream, and the sugar for 1–2 minutes. Stir in the vanilla extract.

Follow your ice cream maker's directions. The ice cream will have a soft, creamy texture. If you prefer a firmer consistency, put the ice cream in an airtight container and place in the freezer for about 2 hours.

Remove from the freezer about 15 minutes before serving.

Makes about 6 cups.

Earl Greater Grey Olive Oil Cake

*K*ate made this cake for us on a sunny afternoon in her beautiful beachside bakery. This cake is like a canvas ready for you to dress it up with your own charms. I like to add drizzles of local Ojai olive oil and a sprinkle of orange blossoms when they are in season.

    3 eggs at room temperature
    ¼ cup vegetable oil
    ½ cup olive oil
    Juice and zest of 2 lemons
    1¼ cups sugar
    2½ cups all-purpose flour, sifted
    1 Zhena's Earl Greater Grey tea sachet

Grease a 9-inch springform pan.
Preheat the oven to 325°.
Using a food processor or an electric mixer, combine the eggs, both oils, and the lemon juice and zest and mix until smooth.
Add the sugar, flour, and tea leaves to the batter and mix until the dry ingredients are thoroughly incorporated.
Place batter in the greased pan and bake for 50 minutes.
Let the cake cool completely before serving. Serve with a fresh pot of Earl Greater Grey for afternoon tea with friends or simply as a treat for yourself as you savor your ability to self-validate a job well done. ☺

Makes 8 slices.

Ultimate Green Tea Madeleines

M adeleines are more cake than cookie. These small treats melt away worry. You can find madeleine pans at any cooking store, such as Williams-Sonoma, or online.

6 tablespoons unsalted butter
2 Zhena's Ultimate Green tea sachets
¾ cup all-purpose flour
½ teaspoon baking powder
2 eggs at room temperature
⅓ cup granulated sugar
2 tablespoons honey
Juice and zest of 1 lemon
2 teaspoons vanilla extract

Melt 5 tablespoons of the butter over low heat in a small pan. Add the tea from the 2 sachets and allow the loose tea to steep in the butter while you make the cookie batter.

Preheat the oven to 350°.

Sift together the flour and baking powder, and set aside.

Using a mixer, beat the eggs, sugar, and honey for 3–5 minutes until tripled in volume.

While the mixer is running, melt 1 tablespoon of butter. Use a pastry brush to paint butter in the madeleine pan, making sure not to let the butter pool. Dust with flour and set aside.

Add the lemon juice and zest and the vanilla to the egg mixture and mix for 1 minute.

With a spatula, fold the flour into the egg mixture, stirring gently until the flour is fully incorporated. Strain the tea butter and fold it into the batter.

Use a tablespoon or pastry bag to fill the madeleine pan. Bake for 12–15 minutes. Then turn the pan upside down and tap it on the counter to release the madeleines.

Serve the cookies within a day for maximum freshness. They are a treat, with hints of lychee, apricot, and the uplifting scent of fresh lemons. Serve with a pot of Ultimate Green Tea and allow the tea and the cakelike cookie to melt in your mouth together, transporting you to a world of carefree moments.

Makes 18 small or 12 large madeleines.

Acknowledgments

I'd like to thank my editor, Leslie Meredith, for believing in me. Leslie's compassion, keen eye and thoughtful care in making suggestions and mindfully editing this book taught me a lot about grace. Thanks to Deb Norton for being the midwife who shaped this book and lovingly coached me every step of the way—this book would not exist without you, my friend. Thank you to Jan Child, whose help and encouragement shepherded the manuscript into its current form and brought me to Atria—I am ever grateful for your friendship and partnership. Great thanks to my publisher, Judith Curr, an amazing visionary. I'm honored to be in your world.

I'd also like to thank my spiritual family at Idulgashinna Tea Estate in Sri Lanka—Alex David, Zaki Alif, Chairman Harry, Gnana Sekram, Manik Jayakumar, and all of the estate workers— this book is for *you*—you are the example of what is possible and beautiful in the world.

To Andrea Rolston, Darakshan Dave Farber, Patty Waltcher, Tom Morehouse, Jim Pallotta, and all of my angel investors who took a chance on me—and my mission—you have made an impact so great that I hope it will inspire millions to buy fair trade tea and maybe even start and grow businesses that heal and change the world.

To my tribe—each employee, supplier, and trading partner past and present—thank you for your love and dedication to the tea and tea workers through the efforts undertaken at Zhena's. Thank you to Paul Rice of Fair Trade USA, the dedicated people of F.L.O., and Demeter USA. Deepest thanks to the P.E.O. and Cottey College—you've taught me the power of a rock-solid, supportive sisterhood.

Thank you to Donna Arrogante for heading up the visual representation of my spirit in the world. Thank you to my New Moon Mastermind Group: Kathy, Kate, Jane, Terri, Donna Dietch, Donna A., Patty, Kathleen, Summers, Lisa, Lori, Kelly, and Liz—you all are my inspiring moon goddesses, and your support is a powerful testament to women supporting other women.

And to my early supporters and believers: Kathleen Coady, Olivia McMullen Fields, Nina Utne, Leigh Haber, and Jan Miller. Your patience and support gave me faith in myself.

Thank you to Leverage Management's Michael Garnett and Audrey Kelly for seeing this book in visual form.

Thanks to Micki for helping in the days of the tea cart, my beautiful mom who worked a second shift to put me through school, my great dad who taught me that work (and fishing) matters, my awesome brothers, Brad and Brian, whose help was the first and most crucial those first days.

And to my husband, Gerard, for loving me through the big ideas that send me to the other side of the world. You are my king, and I promise you'll still be having fun with me in seven lifetimes. ☺

About the Recipes

*K*ate Dunbar and I met five years ago at a keynote for a women's business nonprofit in Santa Barbara, California. She told me that when I was just starting out with the tea cart with my baby on my hip, she was one of the neighborhood hairdressers I made tea lattes for. She approached me after my speech with a beaming, excited idea, and I saw a world of possibility in her bright green eyes.

Her mother is part of a women's organization responsible for educating hundreds of thousands of women. It's called PEO (Philanthropic Educational Organization), and it gave me a scholarship to attend an all-women's college, where we vowed to support and protect other women. What a full circle!

Kate's dream was to be a baker, and as our friendship grew, she was inspired by my tea blends and would stop by our corporate headquarters to drop off amazing treats for my tribe. She formulated baked delights infused with each of my tea blends and soon built a repertoire of recipes. She's been responsible for a lot of fun staff meetings as we munched on her delectable Coconut Chai–infused macaroons and sipped tea, talking about business issues with sugar on our tongues.

Two years ago, Kate and her husband, Steve, joined me in Sri Lanka to visit the tea fields, and as Steve fell in love with the elephants at the elephant orphanage, Kate's love of tea was deepened as she learned the labors of plucking the leaves herself. She texted me from out in the fields and said she was crying because she finally understood the sacred efforts of the adept tea workers whose lives are dedicated to plucking tea while making so very little income. She was always a believer in fair trade, but this created a cathartic experience for her.

Kate and I are "The Baker and the Tea Maker." I'm the Tea Maker, but Kate inspires me. Now I am baking these recipes at home, and my kids, Sage and Mia, LOVE them. Kate is a gift of optimism, dessert, and laughs in my life. You can see me learning how to make these delicious and decadent desserts with her at www.Zhena.tv. Enjoy, and please don't judge my inept baking skills too much! To find Kate, read her blog, and discover more recipes, please go to the same website and click on "The Baker."

Index

257

breathing (*cont.*)
  Sit Steady, Scan, and See exercise
    and, 13–15
Brenda (friend), 177
Brian (market researcher), 58, 61
Buddha
  and living in the present, 15
  and loving-kindness meditation, 90
  and plucking the positive, 75
  Vipassana meditation of, 10–11
burdens
  as blessings, 62–65
  exercise about, 63–65
  Mantra of the Cup and, 62
  and naming of Zhena's company,
    58–61
  repurposing, 63–65
  Yin Zhen and, 56
  and Zhena's founding of company,
    56–61
Buscaglia, Leo, 189
Bush, George W., 121
business cards, 102–3
business plans, 32, 33, 121
business tactics, Zhena's learning about,
  145

café-bookstore
  Zhena as working at, 42
  Zhena's desire to buy, 30–35
cafés, selling Zhena's Gypsy Tea to,
  80–81
caffeine, 68
Camus, Albert, 217
Caramel Chai Panna Cotta (gluten free)
  (recipe), 248
Caramel Chai Tea, 155
Caramelized Pear Biodynamic Tea, 170
cardamom, 42, 98, 143, 222
Carmel-by-the-Sea, 32
carving of the cup
  and answering the call, 141
  benefits of, 230
  exercise for, 12–15
  Mantra of the Cup and, 10
  pain/suffering and, 5, 6–12
  and Tibetan couple, 6–7
celebrating
  benefits of, 163–65, 230
  exercise about, 165–66
  and hosting your own Gypsy Tea
    Party, 231
  success, 162–66
Ceylon black tea, 95, 179

Ceylon orange pekoe, 97
chai
  ingredients for, 96
  See also specific tea
chamomile, 17–18, 23, 95, 169
change
  character and, 167
  pain as messenger of, 10–12
character
  biodynamic products and, 168–76
  change and, 167
  exercise about, 178
  failure/hardship and, 176–77, 178
  Mantra of the Cup and, 176
charity, generosity distinguished from,
  227–28
child labor, 126–27
children
  computer learning center for,
    219–20, 221
  curiosity of, 150
  and modernization of Sri Lanka tea
    estate, 219–20, 221, 223–27
  at New Delhi train station, 126–27,
    130, 134
  of tea workers, 115, 122, 124,
    133–39, 145, 211, 219–20, 221,
    223–27
China, 122, 218
chocolate
  and blending of teas, 97, 98
  in Raspberry Earl Grey Chocolate
    Cupcakes, 244
  in Raspberry Earl Grey Dark Choc-
    olate Ganache Filling, 246
  in Raspberry Earl Grey Dark Choc-
    olate Rum Icing, 244, 245
Chouinard, Yvon, 161
Christmas Tea, 155
cinnamon, 96, 98, 143, 144, 155, 222
Clark, Frank A., 1
Coady, Scott, 113
cocoa, 94–95
Coconut Chai, 143–45, 147–50, 246
Coconut Chai-Infused French Macaroons (recipe), 246
Cody (Meredith's son), illness of, 8–9
Coffee Cat Café (Santa Barbara, California), 149–50
collaboration
  benefits of, 105, 111–15, 230

and difference between Lipton Tea
and Zhena's Gypsy Tea, 108–10
exercise about, 115–17
Mantra of the Cup and, 111
and Raspberry Earl Grey Tea,
106–10
and A Woman's Power Leadership
Project, 113–15
and Zhena's marketing at local spa,
106–10
collagen, Rooibos and, 30
Colombo, Sri Lanka. *See* Sri Lanka
commitment
of Ava to Zhena's Gypsy Tea, 86
importance of, 128
and just showing up, 37, 39
and plucking the positive, 73, 76
of Zhena to Gypsy Tea mission, 212
competition, for Zhena's Gypsy Tea,
156–58, 160–62
computer learning center (Sri Lanka),
219–20, 221
confidence
and just showing up, 37
and starting where you are, 49
control, and asking for help, 24
cups
beauty of, 5
for Gypsy Tea Parties, 235
as inspiration, 5–6
as measure of capacity, 5
and Zhena's signature teacup, 5–6, 9
See also carving of the cup; Mantra
of the Cup
curiosity
benefits of, 230
and Coconut Chai as inspiration,
143–50
cost-cutting and, 146–50
cultivating, 150–51, 152–53
exercise about, 152–53
fear and, 143, 151
Mantra of the Cup and, 150

Daily Show with Jon Stewart (TV program), 111–12
Dalai Lama, 142
Darjeeling teas, 95, 98, 168, 172, 249
dating, Zhena's, 164
Dayan (wedding planner), 204
decisions, making tough, 82–86

Dennard, Ted, 237
Department of Agriculture, US
(USDA), 84
discount stores, Beyond Organic teas
and, 175–76
Disney, Walt, 143
Divine Tea, 119–20
dogs, Lisa's, 88–89
doubt
and just showing up, 37
Rooibos and, 30
dreams
collaboration and, 111
defining, 102
eye contact with, 39
and Gnana's influence on Zhena,
228
Gypsy Tea Parties and, 236
identification of, 38–39
limitations and, 102
perfection and, 49
and plucking the positive, 75, 76
showing up for, 38–39
and starting where you are, 48–54
of tea workers, 137
and visionaries compared with
dreamers, 146
visualizing the reality of, 76
Durga (Sri Lankan student), 134, 221,
224, 226

Earl Greater Grey Olive Oil Cake
(recipe), 250
Earl Greater Grey Tea, 179, 182–84, 250
economy, biodynamic products and,
168–76
Educate Her, Inc., 115
Einstein, Albert, 39, 166
elderberries, 98
Eliot, George, 5
Emerson, Ralph Waldo, 67
Ensler, Eve, 232–33
entrepreneurs
as just showing up, 37
See also specific person
environment, biodynamic farming and,
169
essential oils, 97–98. *See also specific oil*
exercise
Answering the Call, 142
Feedback Forum, 115–17

About the Author

Zhena Muzyka founded Zhena's Gypsy Tea in 2000 to fund her son's lifesaving operations. Celebrated for her work in fair-trade business practices, Zhena's story and products have been featured in *Good Housekeeping, Marie Claire, Inc., Entrepreneur, Woman's World, O: The Oprah Magazine*, the *Los Angeles Times*, and *Every Day with Rachael Ray*, and on the *Dr. Oz Show* and *Good Morning America*. Zhena's honors include the Women Entrepreneur award from *Country Living*, Enterprising Women of the Year Award from *Enterprising Women* magazine, a Socially Responsible Business award, *Pacific Coast Business Times*'s Top Women in Business Award, *Inc.* magazine's 5000 Fastest-Growing Companies, and *Coco Eco* magazine's 20 Most Inspirational Women.

Zhena Muzyka put her background in aromatherapy, a deep love for tea, her Gypsy grandmother's teachings, and a small collection of money from friends and family to work. Embracing her Ukrainian Gypsy ancestry, she began offering her custom teas from a cart on California street corners, believing that selling her tins of tea could alter her fate. It turns out she was right. Today, Zhena's son, Sage, is a healthy fourteen-year-old, and Zhena's Gypsy Tea is a thriving, purpose-driven brand, whose goal is to make a difference in people's lives by offering premium teas and sustainable goods that benefit health, protect the environment, and support humanitarian efforts.

Zhena is focused on helping women build companies that heal and change the world. Zhena spends her time building social mission businesses—cup of tea in hand. She's passionate about writing, traveling, and exploring the world with her family; sourcing and creating sustainable products; building the Robin Hood Laptop Project, which supplies refurbished laptops to the kids in the tea fields and beyond (www.Zhena.tv); consulting, coaching, speaking nationwide to entrepreneurs and corporations, traveling to the tea fields and to Gypsy camps in India, and dreaming up her next book, "Business by the Cup."

You can email her at Zhena@Zhena.tv for inquiries, to learn about her coaching, or book her for speaking. Watch her videos and see her collection of women-centric, mission-driven products at www.Zhena.tv, where you can find jewelry, how-to videos, and blogs, and where you can sign up for her newsletter, which is guaranteed to help you stay infused with inspiration as you take each step toward your dreams.